CONTEMPORARY
FREUD

Turning Points & Critical Issues

ON FREUD'S

"Analysis Terminable and Interminable"

EDITED BY JOSEPH SANDLER

FOR THE INTERNATIONAL

PSYCHOANALYTICAL ASSOCIATION

Yale University Press

New Haven & London

An earlier version of this book, in slightly different form, was
published in a limited, privately distributed, paperback edition by
the International Psychoanalytical Association as *On Freud's
'Analysis Terminable and Interminable,'* copyright © 1987 by
The International Psychoanalytical Association.

Grateful acknowledgment is made to Sigmund Freud Copyrights,
Ltd.; the Institute of Psycho-Analysis, London; the Hogarth Press;
and Basic Books for permission to reprint "Analysis Terminable
and Interminable," as published in Sigmund Freud, *The Standard
Edition of the Complete Works of Sigmund Freud*, vol. 23, trans.
and ed. James Strachey, Hogarth Press, London; and in Sigmund
Freud, *The Collected Papers of Sigmund Freud*, vol. 5, ed. James
Strachey, Basic Books, New York.

Designed by Jill Breitbarth
Set in Times Roman and Optima types by Marathon Typography
Service, Inc., Durham, North Carolina.
Printed in the United States of America.

Library of Congress Cataloging-in-Publication Data
Freud, Sigmund, 1856–1939.
On Freud's "Analysis terminable and interminable" / edited by
Joseph Sandler.
p. cm. — (Contemporary Freud)
Originally published by International Psychoanalytical Association,
© 1987.
Includes bibliographical references and index.
ISBN 0-300-04452-6 (alk. paper)
1. Psychoanalysis. I. Sandler, Joseph. II. Title. III. Series.
RC506.F6985 1991
616.89'17—dc20 90-47986 CIP

The paper in this book meets the guidelines for permanence and
durability of the Committee on Production Guidelines for Book
Longevity of the Council on Library Resources.

2 4 6 8 10 9 7 5 3 1

Contents

Contents / vi

Preface

Psychoanalysis has had the good fortune to be an international discipline almost from its inception, thereby anticipating what has become a global perspective in all areas—intellectual, cultural, and commercial. With the increasingly rapid growth of psychoanalysis in different parts of the world, each with a unique and important focus, the current leadership of the International Psychoanalytical Association (IPA) has looked to new modalities of interchange. To this end the Council of the Association accepted my proposal (in my capacity as chairman of the Publications Committee) for a series of "teaching" volumes with a unique format.

Each of the publications in this series, entitled "Contemporary Freud: Turning Points and Critical Issues," will include one of Freud's classic papers and commentary by a number of distinguished psychoanalytic teachers from diverse theoretical perspectives and national backgrounds who have been asked to shape their discussion as though for presentation in a teaching seminar. To give a coherent picture of each psychoanalytic point of view, contributors not only review the pertinent literature but also provide personal interpretations of the paper in question, elucidating and discussing important points and shedding light on ambiguous passages. They also comment on our present state of knowledge in the area addressed by the classic paper. Each volume of the series is designed for use in teaching, but equally it invites the reader's participation in a very high-level reading group or in a kind of master class.

Because the main topic of the Thirty-Fifth Congress of the IPA was "Analysis Terminable and Interminable: Fifty Years Later," the Publications Committee chose Freud's classic paper of 1937 as the subject of the first volume in this new series. An earlier version of this text was published in paperback and distributed to the membership at the IPA Congress in Montreal in 1987. The time for editorial preparation and translation was necessarily short for the first, limited edition; this Yale publication represents a more fully edited, slightly revised version of the original discussion. There are plans under way to publish this revised edition in the three other official languages of the IPA. The Spanish edition will be published by Technipublicaciones of Madrid.

Three additional papers on the current topic, presented at the Montreal Congress by Didier Anzieu, Harold Blum, and Isadoro Berenstein, have been published previously in English in the *International Journal of Psychoanalysis*, vol. 68, pt. 1, January 1987; in French in the *Revue Francaise de Psychanalyse*, vol. 51, no. 2, Spring 1987; in German in the *Zeitschrift fur psychoanalytishe Theorie und Praxis*, vol. 2, pt. 1, 1987; and in Spanish in the Argentinian *Revista de Psicoanálisis*, vol. 43, pt. 3, 1986.

The second volume, "On Freud's 'On Narcissism: An Introduction,'" will be published in a paperback edition concurrently with the IPA meeting in Argentina in the summer of 1991 and subsequently in a cloth edition by Yale University Press. Beginning with the third volume, hard-cover editions will be distributed at each congress of the IPA. Each volume will be available in all four of the official languages of the IPA: English, French, German, and Spanish.

For assistance in the preparation and editing of this volume, I am grateful to Ethel Person, the current chairperson of the IPA Committee on Publications, and to her two associate chairpersons, Peter Fonagy and Aiban Hagelin. Special thanks are due to Lynne McIlroy for her assistance in coordinating international correspondence and permissions, to Doris Parker for checking the English references, and to Jane Pettit for her invaluable work in proofreading and checking the text. I also want to thank Gladys Topkis and Cynthia Wells of Yale University Press for their perseverance and exactitude in shepherding this volume through to its final form.

JOSEPH SANDLER

Introduction

André Green writes in this volume that "Analysis Terminable and Interminable" "may be regarded as one panel of a triptych which, taken as a whole, forms Freud's testament." This paper is Freud's clinical legacy, accurately summing up his sense of the potential and the limitations of psychoanalysis as a therapeutic technique.

Because a theory of technique must of necessity be related to psychoanalytic theory, different theoretical emphases incline the analyst to particular therapeutic positions. Consequently, psychoanalytic technique and the underlying theory of technique are constantly undergoing minor modifications. Current areas of inquiry focus on the importance of interpreting transference in "the here and now" in addition to (or as opposed to) the reconstruction of the past, the role of insight in change, the nature of therapeutic action, and the concept of therapeutic alliance. There is increasing attention paid to the individual characteristics (including the limitations) of the patient and the psychoanalyst as they influence therapeutic outcome.

A number of these central issues were delineated clearly or at least fore-shadowed in "Analysis Terminable and Interminable." Though many have deemed that paper pessimistic in tone, it might also be lauded for its realism, for its hard-headed look at why the actuality of therapeutic outcome must always fall short of the ideal. It is in this paper that Freud designated psychoanalysis the "impossible" profession (a judgment with which most psychoanalysts seem to concur proudly) and in which he set out to show why this is so.

Freud thoroughly expounds the limitations and impediments to a complete analysis and an ideal termination. He discusses both the formal characteristics of analysis and its ultimate outcome. He acknowledges the desirability of shortening analytic treatment and raises the question of whether such abbreviation is possible—even entertaining the "heroic measure" of setting a firm termination date, although he concludes that the consequences of such a measure appeared to be a limitation on the full analysis of the patient. In the happiest outcome, termination would follow the disappearance of symptoms and the full resolution of the patient's anxieties and inhibitions. Ideally, rather like an inoculation, the concluded analysis also would provide some assurance of protection against a recurrence of illness or the appearance of a new conflict. However, as Freud suggested, the attainment of such "normality" is a fiction, normality being only a statistical concept.

Freud discusses the limitations of analysis in a very systematic way, arguing that the outcome of treatment is ultimately constricted by (1) the constitutionally determined intensity of the patient's drives, (2) the severity of infantile traumas, and (3) the degree of ego distortion produced by defenses. He believed that the intensity of a person's drives was a constitutional given, though drives might undergo intensification or modulation at different stages of life. These purely quantitative factors would affect the capacity of psychoanalysis to help the adult ego to master unconscious conflicts, as psychoanalytic treatment attempts to modify the infantile repression through the confrontation of infantile instinctual conflicts by the more mature ego. But the second two factors, the severity of infantile traumas and the degree of ego distortion, can also place severe limits on what can be achieved in analysis. The ego must of necessity be distorted by the action of its defensive maneuvers, however effective and potentially adaptive they may be. Moreover, constitutionally determined as well as defensively derived ego distortions contribute to the intensity of resistance in the psychoanalytic process.

The "stickiness of the libido" of some patients, the excessive instability of libidinal investments in others, and a general psychic rigidity in still others are all conditions that pose significant impediments to a good analytic outcome. Nor is this an exhaustive list. Freud suggested further obstacles to the completion of an ideal analysis. Widespread masochism, negative therapeutic reactions, and the sense of guilt reported by so many neurotics were, in his view, derivatives—"unmistakable indicators"—of the death instinct. Some patients might even resist recovery itself.

A complicated equilibrium exists between derivatives of the death instincts and libidinal forces. The conflict between these forces, Freud suggests, is the source of resistances and the resulting limitations on treatment. Freud argues that free aggression might contribute to a general disposition to psychic conflict, and as evidence he contrasts those patients in whom there appeared to be an irreducible incompatibility of unconscious homosexual and heterosexual strivings and other (bisexual) patients in whom such strivings coexist without apparent problems. In these discussions, Freud is concerned not just with technical issues but also with the very nature of instincts and of the ego. This manifestly concrete paper on therapeutic technique is in essence a highly metapsychological one.

Freud simultaneously adds that the qualities and skills of the analyst are in themselves significant to analytic outcomes. Though ideally the analyst should continue his or her self-analysis after completion of the personal analysis, more often than not the analyst is too well defended to engage in an effective self-analysis. Therefore Freud recommends reanalysis of the analyst, perhaps at five-year intervals, thus definitively making the analyst's own analysis interminable.

Though an analysis may not be completed, Freud concludes, it must inevitably come to a natural or practical end. And often things go well enough afterwards, even if the ideal was not achieved. Freud ends this discussion by conjuring up the bedrock of resistance to analysis as the inability of women to renounce penis envy and of men to renounce passive or feminine wishes toward other men.

Given that the average analysis today—in spite of its basis in expanded psychoanalytic understanding and its much greater duration—is of equally uncertain outcome to the analyses of Freud's day, his paper must be regarded at the very least as a clear-sighted view of some intransigent barriers to complete analysis that lurk not in technical limitations but in human nature. Our commentators, all distinguished teachers and clinicians, discuss Freud's essay from a multiplicity of viewpoints. They place it in historical perspective, discussing the theoretical and technical questions with which Freud was preoccupied during the period at which he wrote it. They frame Freud's insights and observations within the major theoretical questions of the period and within contemporary concerns. Of particular interest is the slightly different theoretical focus of each of our commentators.

Jacob Arlow opens the discussion by emphasizing that because any theory of technique must be related to a particular concept of pathological process, having a coherent and consistent conceptual model is crucial. He observes that in "Analysis Terminable and Interminable," Freud's summing-up paper on technique, Freud was fluctuating between his earlier, topographic and later, structural models. Arlow argues that because it was hard for Freud to give up the topographical point of view, he overemphasized the curative potential of recovering memories and focused merely on undoing repression. Using this contention as a point of departure, he explains how technique now is understood within the structural framework of ego psychology. He elaborates on differences in the way the transference is regarded from the structural point of view and the variety of clinical explanations—as opposed to the metapsychological ones Freud invoked—that can account for the limits to complete analysis. He alludes to the multiplicity of specific transference fantasies common to the termination phase of analysis. He concludes that belief in a prophylactic immunization against neurosis is itself a magical fantasy and suggests that those analysts who subscribe to the conflictual point of view are perhaps better able than others to form a realistic view of the outcome of analysis.

Harald Leupold-Löwenthal's chapter, originally written in German, is an important historical contribution. An extremely scholarly treatment of "Analysis Terminable and Interminable," it helps us understand the large theoretical implications of Freud's paper beyond its specific assessment of the therapeutic results of analysis. Drawing on the whole corpus of Freud's work as well as on relevant comments by others in the field, Leupold-Löwenthal discusses both Freud's treatment of ego development and his belief in the death instinct. Most important, he considers the implications of Freud's argument that the analyst's own analysis must constantly be renewed.

In their thorough exegesis of "Analysis Terminable and Interminable," David Zimmermann and A. L. Bento Mostardeiro describe Freud's professional and personal situations during the writing of the paper, discuss the basic therapeutic issues it addresses, and do an in-depth analysis of central subtopics in the paper, including assessing terminability, the source of structural variations in the ego, and the analyst's repudiation of femininity.

Terttu Eskelinen de Folch starts with the proposition that, thanks to new developments in analytic technique, we can now treat patients analytically who would have been inaccessible to us in the past. In acknowledging that we still face the same limitations to complete analysis mentioned by Freud, she proposes a few new explanations. In particular she focuses on what she calls "concealed nuclei of the personality," which in some patients can cause acute difficulty in recognizing and confronting the destructive impulses of hatred and envy. Eskelinen de Folch argues that, contrary to some analysts' expectations, these nuclei do appear in the transference in the object relation with the analyst, and she presents some clinical material to support this point of view. She utilizes Melanie Klein's concepts of projective identification and her theory of the paranoid schizoid position with a discussion of the technical problems involved when the analyst addresses issues of splitting and projective identification. In elucidating these issues she draws upon the theory of the death instinct and the repetition compulsion. This chapter has been translated from the original Spanish.

Arnold Cooper, like Arlow, emphasizes the fluctuations in "Analysis Terminable and Interminable" between ego psychology and topographical theory, but he takes this observation in a different direction from Arlow's formulation. He argues that our ideas about the concepts of "instinct taming" are considerably changed from Freud's day, the contemporary focus having shifted toward an interpersonal and object relational point of view. As he puts it, the "unit under study in a very young infant is the infant-mother pair, not the infant alone." In such a view one cannot quantify instinct, "since whatever is constitutional always and immediately interacts with behaviors of the caretaker toward the expression of those tendencies." Cooper's solution to this problem is to postulate tensions resulting from dysphoric affects rather than from instincts. Analogously, he proposes that much of our current thinking on cure derives from Strachey's paper in which it is suggested that the real agent of cure is not the lifting of repression but the patient's internalization of aspects of the analyst. Here again Cooper focuses on the mental structure of object representations. Overall he suggests that Freud relied too much on metapsychology, too little on clinical theory and that he wrongly invoked biology—the repudiation of femininity—as the irreducible obstacle to a complete therapeutic outcome. Finally he discusses narrative construction and the hermeneutic view in relationship to technical questions. Using this model he finds himself in agreement with Freud that the process of analysis is interminable, but for a reason—"the human personality is constantly re-creating itself" — that differs from Freud's explanation.

The role of instinct in Freud's paper is the subject of André Green's chapter, here translated from the French. He discusses the ways in which the concept of instinct has been rejected or revised in different analytic schools of thought. He argues that some of Freud's ideas are too metaphysical for today's psychoanalytic world. Nonetheless, in basic agreement with Freud, he concludes "these hypotheses appear only as generalizations derived from *observation of the most trivial facts of existence*. This is proved by the examples Freud uses as evidence in his paper. There is nothing that does not allude to the most common relations that link human beings together. Those who scorn these speculations take care not to advance others with equivalent or superior explanatory ability." Textual analysis of Freud reveals "an important semantic shift whereby, in our view, the object — through the explicit reference to a love instinct — is accorded a position of paramount importance compared with its situation in the earlier instinctual theories — namely, the theories of the sexual instinct." For Green, the object is the agent that reveals the instinct, a conclusion he reaches through careful theoretical reasoning. He uses this as a segue toward establishing a line of development between instinct and language.

In the final commentary, translated from the Spanish, Rosenfeld explores ideas stimulated by Freud's paper through the device of an imaginary conversation carried on among four individuals, a moderator and three students, each of whom represents a different mode, or phase, of learning. One character in the imaginary exchange is striving for a stable theory, another for the capacity to have humility in the face of not knowing, and the third is expressing a new approach. This device enables Rosenfeld to show connections between some of Freud's ideas and later developments as formulated by Heinz Hartmann, by Anna Freud, and by Harold Blum. All in all, his is a wide-ranging treatment of the issues, which also includes a discussion of the effect of cultural conditions on the analytic situation and on theory and a plea for openness and enough flexibility to modify theory. It is a charming and appropriate end to a volume that brings together diverse, sometimes contradictory but always enlightening discussions of Freud's views and our contemporaries' views on both the triumphs and limitations of analysis.

JOSEPH SANDLER
ETHEL PERSON
PETER FONAGY

PART ONE

Analysis Terminable
and Interminable (1937)

SIGMUND FREUD

ANALYSIS TERMINABLE AND INTERMINABLE

I

EXPERIENCE has taught us that psycho-analytic therapy—the freeing of someone from his neurotic symptoms, inhibitions and abnormalities of character—is a time-consuming business. Hence, from the very first, attempts have been made to shorten the duration of analyses. Such endeavours required no justification; they could claim to be based on the strongest considerations of reason and expediency. But there was probably still at work in them as well some trace of the impatient contempt with which the medical science of an earlier day regarded the neuroses as being uncalled-for consequences of invisible injuries. If it had now become necessary to attend to them, they should at least be disposed of as quickly as possible.

A particularly energetic attempt in this direction was made by Otto Rank, following upon his book, *The Trauma of Birth* (1924). He supposed that the true source of neurosis was the act of birth, since this involves the possibility of a child's 'primal fixation' to his mother not being surmounted but persisting as a 'primal repression'. Rank hoped that if this primal trauma were dealt with by a subsequent analysis the whole neurosis would be got rid of. Thus this one small piece of analytic work would save the necessity for all the rest. And a few months should be enough to accomplish this. It cannot be disputed that Rank's argument was bold and ingenious; but it did not stand the test of critical examination. Moreover, it was a child of its time, conceived under the stress of the contrast between the post-war misery of Europe and the 'prosperity' [1] of America, and designed to adapt the tempo of analytic therapy to the haste of American life. We have not heard much about what the implementation of Rank's plan has done for cases of sickness. Probably not more than if the fire-brigade, called to deal with a house that had been set on fire by an overturned oil-lamp, contented themselves with removing the lamp from the room

---

[1] [In English in the original.]

in which the blaze had started. No doubt a considerable shortening of the brigade's activities would be effected by this means. The theory and practice of Rank's experiment are now things of the past—no less than American 'prosperity' itself.[1]

I myself had adopted another way of speeding up an analytic treatment even before the war. At that time I had taken on the case of a young Russian, a man spoilt by wealth, who had come to Vienna in a state of complete helplessness, accompanied by a private doctor and an attendant.[2] In the course of a few years it was possible to give him back a large amount of his independence, to awaken his interest in life and to adjust his relations to the people most important to him. But there progress came to a stop. We advanced no further in clearing up the neurosis of his childhood, on which his later illness was based, and it was obvious that the patient found his present position highly comfortable and had no wish to take any step forward which would bring him nearer to the end of his treatment. It was a case of the treatment inhibiting itself: it was in danger of failing as a result of its—partial—success. In this predicament I resorted to the heroic measure of fixing a time-limit for the analysis.[3] At the beginning of a year's work I informed the patient that the coming year was to be the last one of his treatment, no matter what he achieved in the time still left to him. At first he did not believe me, but once he was convinced that I was in deadly earnest, the desired change set in. His resistances shrank up, and in these last months of his treatment he was able to reproduce all the memories and to discover all the connections which seemed necessary for understanding his early neurosis and mastering his present one. When he left me in the midsummer of 1914, with as little suspicion as the rest of us of what lay so shortly ahead, I believed that his cure was radical and permanent.

In a footnote added to this patient's case history in 1923,[4]

[1] [This was written soon after the great financial crisis in the United States. A considered criticism of Rank's theory had been given by Freud in *Inhibitions, Symptoms and Anxiety* (1926*d*). See, in particular, *Standard Ed.*, **20**, 135–6 and 150–3.]

[2] See my paper, published with the patient's consent, 'From the History of an Infantile Neurosis' (1918*b*). It contains no detailed account of the young man's adult illness, which is touched on only when its connection with his infantile neurosis absolutely requires it.

[3] [See *Standard Ed.*, **17**, 10–11.]　　　　[4] [Ibid., 121.]

I have already reported that I was mistaken. When, towards the end of the war, he returned to Vienna, a refugee and destitute, I had to help him to master a part of the transference which had not been resolved. This was accomplished in a few months, and I was able to end my footnote with the statement that 'since then the patient has felt normal and has behaved unexceptionably, in spite of the war having robbed him of his home, his possessions, and all his family relationships'. Fifteen years have passed since then without disproving the truth of this verdict; but certain reservations have become necessary. The patient has stayed on in Vienna and has kept a place in society, if a humble one. But several times during this period his good state of health has been interrupted by attacks of illness which could only be construed as offshoots of his perennial neurosis. Thanks to the skill of one of my pupils, Dr. Ruth Mack Brunswick, a short course of treatment has on each occasion brought these conditions to an end. I hope that Dr. Mack Brunswick herself will shortly report on the circumstances.[1] Some of these attacks were still concerned with residual portions of the transference; and, where this was so, short-lived though they were, they showed a distinctly paranoid character. In other attacks, however, the pathogenic material consisted of pieces of the patient's childhood history, which had not come to light while I was analysing him and which now came away—the comparison is unavoidable—like sutures after . an operation, or small fragments of necrotic bone. I have found the history of this patient's recovery scarcely less interesting than that of his illness.

I have subsequently employed this fixing of a time-limit in other cases as well, and I have also taken the experiences of other analysts into account. There can be only one verdict about the value of this blackmailing device: it is effective provided that one hits the right time for it. But it cannot guarantee to accomplish the task completely. On the contrary, we may be sure that, while part of the material will become accessible under the pressure of the threat, another part will be kept back and thus become buried, as it were, and lost to our therapeutic efforts. For once the analyst has fixed the time-limit he cannot

[1] [Her report had in fact already appeared several years earlier (Brunswick, 1928). For further information on the later history of the case see an editorial footnote, *Standard Ed.*, **17**, 122.]

extend it; otherwise the patient would lose all faith in him. The most obvious way out would be for the patient to continue his treatment with another analyst, although we know that such a change will involve a fresh loss of time and abandoning fruits of work already done. Nor can any general rule be laid down as to the right time for resorting to this forcible technical device; the decision must be left to the analyst's tact. A miscalculation cannot be rectified. The saying that a lion only springs once must apply here.

II

The discussion of the technical problem of how to accelerate the slow progress of an analysis leads us to another, more deeply interesting question: is there such a thing as a natural end to an analysis—is there any possibility at all of bringing an analysis to such an end? To judge by the common talk of analysts it would seem to be so, for we often hear them say, when they are deploring or excusing the recognized imperfections of some fellow-mortal: 'His analysis was not finished' or 'he was never analysed to the end.'

We must first of all decide what is meant by the ambiguous phrase 'the end of an analysis'. From a practical standpoint it is easy to answer. An analysis is ended when the analyst and the patient cease to meet each other for the analytic session. This happens when two conditions have been approximately fulfilled: first, that the patient shall no longer be suffering from his symptoms and shall have overcome his anxieties and his inhibitions; and secondly, that the analyst shall judge that so much repressed material has been made conscious, so much that was unintelligible has been explained, and so much internal resistance conquered, that there is no need to fear a repetition of the pathological processes concerned. If one is prevented by external difficulties from reaching this goal, it is better to speak of an *incomplete* analysis rather than of an *unfinished* one.

The other meaning of the 'end' of an analysis is much more ambitious. In this sense of it, what we are asking is whether the analyst has had such a far-reaching influence on the patient that no further change could be expected to take place in him if his analysis were continued. It is as though it were possible by means of analysis to attain to a level of absolute psychical

normality—a level, moreover, which we could feel confident
would be able to remain stable, as though, perhaps, we had
succeeded in resolving every one of the patient's repressions and
in filling in all the gaps in his memory. We may first consult our
experience to enquire whether such things do in fact happen,
and then turn to our theory to discover whether there is any
possibility of their happening.

Every analyst will have treated a few cases which have had
this gratifying outcome. He has succeeded in clearing up the
patient's neurotic disturbance, and it has not returned and has
not been replaced by any other such disturbance. Nor are we
without some insight into the determinants of these successes.
The patient's ego had not been noticeably altered[1] and the
aetiology of his disturbance had been essentially traumatic. The
aetiology of every neurotic disturbance is, after all, a mixed
one. It is a question either of the instincts being excessively
strong—that is to say, recalcitrant to taming[2] by the ego—or of
the effects of early (i.e. premature) traumas which the immature
ego was unable to master. As a rule there is a combination of
both factors, the constitutional and the accidental. The stronger
the constitutional factor, the more readily will a trauma lead
to a fixation and leave behind a developmental disturbance; the
stronger the trauma, the more certainly will its injurious effects
become manifest even when the instinctual situation is normal.
There is no doubt that an aetiology of the traumatic sort offers
by far the more favourable field for analysis. Only when a case
is a predominantly traumatic one will analysis succeed in doing
what it is so superlatively able to do; only then will it, thanks
to having strengthened the patient's ego, succeed in replacing
by a correct solution the inadequate decision made in his early
life. Only in such cases can one speak of an analysis having
been definitively ended. In them, analysis has done all that it
should and does not need to be continued. It is true that, if the
patient who has been restored in this way never produces
another disorder calling for analysis, we do not know how much
his immunity may not be due to a kind fate which has spared
him ordeals that are too severe.

A constitutional strength of instinct and an unfavourable

[1] [The idea of an 'alteration of the ego' is discussed at length below,
particularly in Section V. See also the Editor's Note, p. 212 f. above.]
[2] [This word is considered below, on p. 225.]

alteration of the ego acquired in its defensive struggle in the sense of its being dislocated and restricted—these are the factors which are prejudicial to the effectiveness of analysis and which may make its duration interminable. One is tempted to make the first factor—strength of instinct—responsible as well for the emergence of the second—the alteration of the ego; but it seems that the latter too has an aetiology of its own. And, indeed, it must be admitted that our knowledge of these matters is as yet insufficient. They are only now becoming the subject of analytic study. In this field the interest of analysts seems to me to be quite wrongly directed. Instead of an enquiry into how a cure by analysis comes about (a matter which I think has been sufficiently elucidated) the question should be asked of what are the obstacles that stand in the way of such a cure.

This brings me to two problems which arise directly out of analytic practice, as I hope to show by the following examples. A certain man, who had himself practised analysis with great success, came to the conclusion that his relations both to men and women—to the men who were his competitors and to the woman whom he loved—were nevertheless not free from neurotic impediments; and he therefore made himself the subject of an analysis by someone else whom he regarded as superior to himself.[1] This critical illumination of his own self had a completely successful result. He married the woman he loved and turned into a friend and teacher of his supposed rivals. Many years passed in this way, during which his relations with his former analyst also remained unclouded. But then, for no assignable external reason, trouble arose. The man who had been analysed became antagonistic to the analyst and reproached him for having failed to give him a complete analysis. The analyst, he said, ought to have known and to have taken into account the fact that a transference-relation can never be purely positive; he should have given his attention to the possibilities of a negative transference. The analyst defended himself by saying that, at the time of the analysis, there was no sign of a negative transference. But even if he had failed to observe

[1] [According to Ernest Jones this relates to Ferenczi, who was analysed by Freud for three weeks in October, 1914, and for another three weeks (with two sessions daily) in June, 1916. See Jones, 1957, 158, and 1955, 195 and 213. Cf. also Freud's obituary of Ferenczi (1933c), *Standard Ed.*, **22**, 228.]

some very faint signs of it—which was not altogether ruled out, considering the limited horizon of analysis in those early days —it was still doubtful, he thought, whether he would have had the power to activate a topic (or, as we say, a 'complex') by merely pointing it out, so long as it was not currently active in the patient himself at the time. To activate it would certainly have required some unfriendly piece of behaviour in reality on the analyst's part. Furthermore, he added, not every good relation between an analyst and his subject during and after analysis was to be regarded as a transference; there were also friendly relations which were based on reality and which proved to be viable.

I now pass on to my second example, which raises the same problem. An unmarried woman, no longer young, had been cut off from life since puberty by an inability to walk, owing to severe pains in the legs. Her condition was obviously of a hysterical nature, and it had defied many kinds of treatment. An analysis lasting three-quarters of a year removed the trouble and restored to the patient, an excellent and worthy person, her right to a share in life. In the years following her recovery she was consistently unfortunate. There were disasters in her family, and financial losses, and, as she grew older, she saw every hope of happiness in love and marriage vanish. But the one-time invalid stood up to all this valiantly and was a support to her family in difficult times. I cannot remember whether it was twelve or fourteen years after the end of her analysis that, owing to profuse haemorrhages, she was obliged to undergo a gynaecological examination. A myoma was found, which made a complete hysterectomy advisable. From the time of this operation, the woman became ill once more. She fell in love with her surgeon, wallowed in masochistic phantasies about the fearful changes in her inside—phantasies with which she concealed her romance—and proved inaccessible to a further attempt at analysis. She remained abnormal to the end of her life. The successful analytic treatment took place so long ago that we cannot expect too much from it; it was in the earliest years of my work as an analyst. No doubt the patient's second illness may have sprung from the same source as her first one which had been successfully overcome: it may have been a different manifestation of the same repressed impulses, which the analysis had only incompletely resolved. But I am inclined to think that, were it not for the new trauma, there would have been no fresh outbreak of neurosis.

These two examples, which have been purposely selected from a large number of similar ones, will suffice to start a discussion of the topics we are considering. The sceptical, the optimistic and the ambitious will take quite different views of them. The first will say that it is now proved that even a successful analytic treatment does not protect the patient, who at the time has been cured, from falling ill later on of another neurosis—or, indeed, of a neurosis derived from the same instinctual root—that is to say, from a recurrence of his old trouble. The others will consider that this is not proved. They will object that the two examples date from the early days of analysis, twenty and thirty years ago, respectively; and that since then we have acquired deeper insight and wider knowledge, and that our technique has changed in accordance with our new discoveries. To-day, they will say, we may demand and expect that an analytic cure shall prove permanent, or at least that if a patient falls ill again, his new illness shall not turn out to be a revival of his earlier instinctual disturbance, manifesting itself in new forms. Our experience, they will maintain, does not oblige us to restrict so materially the demands that can be made upon our therapeutic method.

My reason for choosing these two examples is, of course, precisely because they lie so far back in the past. It is obvious that the more recent the successful outcome of an analysis is, the less utilizable it is for our discussion, since we have no means of predicting what the later history of the recovery will be. The optimists' expectations clearly presuppose a number of things which are not precisely self-evident. They assume, firstly, that there really is a possibility of disposing of an instinctual conflict (or, more correctly, a conflict between the ego and an instinct) definitively and for all time; secondly, that while we are treating someone for one instinctual conflict we can, as it were, inoculate him against the possibility of any other such conflicts; and thirdly, that we have the power, for purposes of prophylaxis, to stir up a pathogenic conflict of this sort which is not betraying itself at the time by any indications, and that it is wise to do so. I throw out these questions without proposing to answer them now. Perhaps it may not be possible at present to give any certain answer to them at all.

Some light may probably be thrown on them by theoretical considerations. But another point has already become clear: if we wish to fulfil the more exacting demands upon analytic therapy, our road will not lead us to, or by way of, a shortening of its duration.

III

An analytic experience which now extends over several decades, and a change which has taken place in the nature and mode of my activity, encourage me to attempt to answer the questions before us. In earlier days I treated quite a large number of patients, who, as was natural, wanted to be dealt with as quickly as possible. Of late years I have been mainly engaged in training analyses; a relatively small number of severe cases of illness remained with me for continuous treatment, interrupted, however, by longer or shorter intervals. With them, the therapeutic aim was no longer the same. There was no question of shortening the treatment; the purpose was radically to exhaust the possibilities of illness in them and to bring about a deep-going alteration of their personality.

Of the three factors which we have recognized as being decisive for the success or otherwise of analytic treatment—the influence of traumas, the constitutional strength of the instincts and alterations of the ego—what concerns us here is only the second, the strength of the instincts. A moment's reflection raises a doubt whether the restrictive use of the adjective 'constitutional' (or 'congenital') is essential. However true it may be that the constitutional factor is of decisive importance from the very beginning, it is nevertheless conceivable that a reinforcement of instinct coming later in life might produce the same effects. If so, we should have to modify our formula and say 'the strength of the instincts *at the time*' instead of 'the *constitutional* strength of the instincts'. The first of our questions [p. 223] was: 'Is it possible by means of analytic therapy to dispose of a conflict between an instinct and the ego, or of a pathogenic instinctual demand upon the ego, permanently and definitively?' To avoid misunderstanding it is not unnecessary, perhaps, to explain more exactly what is meant by 'permanently disposing of an instinctual demand'. Certainly not 'causing the demand to disappear so that nothing more is ever heard from it again'. This is in general impossible, nor is it at all to be desired. No, we mean something else, something which may be roughly described as a 'taming'[1] of the instinct. That is to say, the instinct is brought completely into the harmony of the ego, becomes accessible to all the influences of the other trends in the ego and no longer seeks to go its independent way to satisfaction. If we are asked by what methods and means this result is achieved, it is not easy to find an answer. We can only say: 'So muss denn doch die Hexe dran!'[2]—the Witch Metapsychology. Without metapsychological speculation and theorizing—I had almost said 'phantasying'—we shall not get another step forward. Unfortunately, here as elsewhere, what our Witch reveals is neither very clear nor very detailed. We have only a single clue to start from—though it is a clue of the highest value—namely, the antithesis between the primary and the secondary processes; and to that antithesis I shall at this point turn.

If now we take up our first question once more, we find that our new line of approach inevitably leads us to a particular conclusion. The question was whether it is possible to dispose of an instinctual conflict permanently and definitively—i.e. to 'tame' an instinctual demand in that fashion. Formulated in these terms, the question makes no mention at all of the strength of the instinct; but it is precisely on this that the outcome depends. Let us start from the assumption that what analysis achieves for neurotics is nothing other than what normal people bring about for themselves without its help. Everyday experience, however, teaches us that in a normal person any solution of an instinctual conflict only holds good for a particular strength of instinct, or, more correctly, only for a particular relation between the strength of the instinct and the strength

---

[1] ['*Bändigung.*' Freud had, among other places, used the word in 'The Economic Problem of Masochism' (1924c) to describe the action by which the libido can make the death instinct innocuous, *Standard Ed.*, **19**, 164. Much earlier, in Section 3 of Part III of the 'Project' of 1895, he had used it of the process by which painful memories cease to carry affect, owing to the intervention of the ego. (Freud, 1950a.)]

[2] ['We must call the Witch to our help after all!'
Goethe, *Faust*, Part I, Scene 6.'
Faust, in search of the secret of youth, unwillingly seeks for the Witch's help.]

of the ego.[1] If the strength of the ego diminishes, whether through illness or exhaustion, or from some similar cause, all the instincts which have so far been successfully tamed may renew their demands and strive to obtain substitutive satisfactions in abnormal ways.[2] Irrefutable proof of this statement is supplied by our nightly dreams; they react to the sleeping attitude assumed by the ego with an awakening of instinctual demands.

The material on the other side [the strength of the instincts] is equally unambiguous. Twice in the course of individual development certain instincts are considerably reinforced: at puberty, and, in women, at the menopause. We are not in the least surprised if a person who was not neurotic before becomes so at these times. When his instincts were not so strong, he succeeded in taming them; but when they are reinforced he can no longer do so. The repressions behave like dams against the pressure of water. The same effects which are produced by these two physiological reinforcements of instinct, may be brought about in an irregular fashion by accidental causes at any other period of life. Such reinforcements may be set up by fresh traumas, enforced frustrations, or the collateral influence of instincts upon one another. The result is always the same, and it underlines the irresistible power of the quantitative factor in the causation of illness.

I feel as though I ought to be ashamed of so much ponderous exposition, seeing that everything I have said has long been familiar and self-evident. It is a fact that we have always behaved as if we knew all this; but, for the most part, our theoretical concepts have neglected to attach the same importance to the *economic* line of approach as they have to the

[1] Or, to be perfectly accurate, where that relation falls within certain limits.

[2] Here we have a justification of the claim to aetiological importance of such non-specific factors as overwork, shock, etc. These factors have always been assured of general recognition, but have had to be pushed into the background precisely by psycho-analysis. It is impossible to define health except in metapsychological terms: i.e. by reference to the dynamic relations between the agencies of the mental apparatus which have been recognized—or (if that is preferred) inferred or conjectured—by us. [Early depreciation by Freud of the aetiological importance in neurosis of such factors as 'overwork' will be found as early as in Draft A in the Fliess papers, dating perhaps from 1892 (1950a, *Standard Ed.*, 1).]

dynamic and *topographical* ones. My excuse is therefore that I am drawing attention to this neglect.[1]

Before we decide on an answer to this question, however, we must consider an objection whose force lies in the fact that we are probably predisposed in its favour. Our arguments, it will be said, are all deduced from the processes which take place spontaneously between the ego and the instincts, and they presuppose that analytic therapy can accomplish nothing which does not, under favourable and normal conditions, occur of itself. But is this really so? Is it not precisely the claim of our theory that analysis produces a state which never does arise spontaneously in the ego and that this newly created state constitutes the essential difference between a person who has been analysed and a person who has not? Let us bear in mind what this claim is based on. All repressions take place in early childhood; they are primitive defensive measures taken by the immature, feeble ego. In later years no fresh repressions are carried out; but the old ones persist, and their services continue to be made use of by the ego for mastering the instincts. New conflicts are disposed of by what we call 'after-repression'.[2] We may apply to these infantile repressions our general statement that repressions depend absolutely and entirely on the relative strength of the forces involved and that they cannot hold out against an increase in the strength of the instincts. Analysis, however, enables the ego, which has attained greater maturity and strength, to undertake a revision of these old repressions; a few are demolished, while others are recognized but constructed afresh out of more solid material. These new dams are of quite a different degree of firmness from the earlier ones; we may be confident that they will not give way so easily before a rising flood of instinctual strength. Thus the real achievement of analytic therapy would be the subsequent correction of the original process of repression, a correction which puts an end to the dominance of the quantitative factor.

Thus far our theory, which we cannot give up except under

[1] [This same line of argument had been traced particularly clearly, in less technical language, in Chapter VII of *The Question of Lay Analysis* (1926*e*), *Standard Ed.*, **20**, 241–3.]

[2] ['*Nachverdrängung*.' See the metapsychological paper on 'Repression' (1915*d*), *Standard Ed.*, **14**, 148, where, however, (as elsewhere at that period) the term used is '*Nachdrängen*', translated 'after-pressure'.]

irresistible compulsion. And what does our *experience* have to say to this? Perhaps our experience is not yet wide enough for us to come to a settled conclusion. It confirms our expectations often enough, but not always. One has an impression that one ought not to be surprised if it should turn out in the end that the difference between a person who has not been analysed and the behaviour of a person after he has been analysed is not so thorough-going as we aim at making it and as we expect and maintain it to be. If this is so, it would mean that analysis *sometimes* succeeds in eliminating the influence of an increase in instinct, but not invariably, or that the effect of analysis is limited to increasing the power of resistance of the inhibitions, so that they are equal to much greater demands than before the analysis or if no analysis had taken place. I really cannot commit myself to a decision on this point, nor do I know whether a decision is possible at the present time.

There is, however, another angle from which we can approach this problem of the variability in the effect of analysis. We know that the first step towards attaining intellectual mastery of our environment is to discover generalizations, rules and laws which bring order into chaos. In doing this we simplify the world of phenomena; but we cannot avoid falsifying it, especially if we are dealing with processes of development and change. What we are concerned with is discerning a *qualitative* alteration, and as a rule in doing so we neglect, at any rate to begin with, a *quantitative* factor. In the real world, transitions and intermediate stages are far more common than sharply differentiated opposite states. In studying developments and changes we direct our attention solely to the outcome; we readily overlook the fact that such processes are usually more or less incomplete—that is to say, that they are in fact only partial alterations. A shrewd satirist of old Austria, Johann Nestroy,[1] once said: 'Every step forward is only half as big as it looks at first.' It is tempting to attribute a quite general validity to this malicious dictum. There are nearly always residual phenomena, a partial hanging-back. When an open-handed Maecenas surprises us by some isolated trait of miserliness, or when a person who is consistently over-kind suddenly indulges in a hostile action, such 'residual phenomena' are

---

[1] [Freud had quoted the same remark in *The Question of Lay Analysis* (1926e), *Standard Ed.*, **20**, 193.]

invaluable for genetic research. They show us that these praise-worthy and precious qualities are based on compensation and overcompensation which, as was to have been expected, have not been absolutely and fully successful. Our first account of the development of the libido was that an original oral phase gave way to a sadistic-anal phase and that this was in turn succeeded by a phallic-genital one. Later research has not contradicted this view, but it has corrected it by adding that these replace-ments do not take place all of a sudden but gradually, so that portions of the earlier organization always persist alongside of the more recent one, and even in normal development the transformation is never complete and residues of earlier libidinal fixations may still be retained in the final configuration. The same thing is to be seen in quite other fields. Of all the erroneous and superstitious beliefs of mankind that have supposedly been surmounted there is not one whose residues do not live on among us to-day in the lower strata of civilized peoples or even in the highest strata of cultural society. What has once come to life clings tenaciously to its existence. One feels inclined to doubt sometimes whether the dragons of primaeval days are really extinct.

Applying these remarks to our present problem, I think that the answer to the question of how to explain the variable results of our analytic therapy might well be that we, too, in endeavouring to replace repressions that are insecure by reliable ego-syntonic controls, do not always achieve our aim to its full extent—that is, do not achieve it thoroughly enough. The transformation is achieved, but often only partially: portions of the old mechanisms remain untouched by the work of analysis. It is difficult to prove that this is really so; for we have no other way of judging what happens but by the outcome which we are trying to explain. Nevertheless, the impressions one receives during the work of analysis do not contradict this assumption; indeed, they seem rather to confirm it. But we must not take the clarity of our own insight as a measure of the conviction which we produce in the patient. His conviction may lack 'depth', as one might say; it is always a question of the quantita-tive factor, which is so easily overlooked. If this is the correct answer to our question, we may say that analysis, in claiming to cure neuroses by ensuring control over instinct, is always right in theory but not always right in practice. And this is because it does not always succeed in ensuring to a sufficient degree the foundations on which a control of instinct is based. The cause of such a partial failure is easily discovered. In the past, the quantitative factor of instinctual strength opposed the ego's defensive efforts; for that reason we called in the work of analysis to help; and now that same factor sets a limit to the efficacy of this new effort. If the strength of the instinct is excessive, the mature ego, supported by analysis, fails in its task, just as the helpless ego failed formerly. Its control over instinct is improved, but it remains imperfect because the transformation in the defensive mechanism is only incomplete. There is nothing surprising in this, since the power of the instruments with which analysis operates is not unlimited but restricted, and the final upshot always depends on the relative strength of the psychical agencies which are struggling with one another.

No doubt it is desirable to shorten the duration of analytic treatment, but we can only achieve our therapeutic purpose by increasing the power of analysis to come to the assistance of the ego. Hypnotic influence seemed to be an excellent instrument for our purposes; but the reasons for our having to abandon it are well known. No substitute for hypnosis has yet been found. From this point of view we can understand how such a master of analysis as Ferenczi came to devote the last years of his life to therapeutic experiments, which, unhappily, proved to be vain.

IV

The two further questions—whether, while we are treating one instinctual conflict, we can protect a patient from future conflicts, and whether it is feasible and expedient, for prophylactic purposes, to stir up a conflict which is not at the time manifest—must be treated together; for obviously the first task can only be carried out in so far as the second one is—that is, in so far as a possible future conflict is turned into an actual present one upon which influence is then brought to bear. This new way of stating the problem is at bottom only an extension of the earlier one. Whereas in the first instance we were considering how to guard against a return of the same conflict, we are now considering how to guard against its possible replacement by *another* conflict. This sounds a very ambitious proposal, but all we are trying to do is to make clear what limits are set to the efficacy of analytic therapy.

However much our therapeutic ambition may be tempted to undertake such tasks, experience flatly rejects the notion. If an instinctual conflict is not a currently active one, is not manifesting itself, we cannot influence it even by analysis. The warning that we should let sleeping dogs lie, which we have so often heard in connection with our efforts to explore the psychical underworld, is peculiarly inapposite when applied to the conditions of mental life. For if the instincts are causing disturbances, it is a proof that the dogs are not sleeping; and if they seem really to be sleeping, it is not in our power to awaken them. This last statement, however, does not seem to be quite accurate and calls for a more detailed discussion. Let us consider what means we have at our disposal for turning an instinctual conflict which is at the moment latent into one which is currently active. Obviously there are only two things that we can do. We can bring about situations in which the conflict does become currently active, or we can content ourselves with discussing it in the analysis and pointing out the possibility of its arising. The first of these two alternatives can be carried out in two ways: in reality, or in the transference—in either case by exposing the patient to a certain amount of real suffering through frustration and the damming up of libido. Now it is true that we already make use of a technique of this kind in our ordinary analytic procedure. What would otherwise be the meaning of the rule that analysis must be carried out 'in a state of frustration'?[1] But this is a technique which we use in treating a conflict which is already currently active. We seek to bring this conflict to a head, to develop it to its highest pitch, in order to increase the instinctual force available for its solution. Analytic experience has taught us that the better is always the enemy of the good[2] and that in every phase of the patient's recovery we have to fight against his inertia, which is ready to be content with an incomplete solution.

If, however, what we are aiming at is a prophylactic treatment of instinctual conflicts that are not currently active but merely potential, it will not be enough to regulate sufferings

[1] [See the paper on 'Transference Love' (1915a), *Standard Ed.*, **12**, 165 and the Budapest Congress paper (1919a), ibid., **17**, 162 ff.]

[2] [The French proverb: '*le mieux est l'ennemi du bien.*']

which are already present in the patient and which he cannot avoid. We should have to make up our minds to provoke fresh sufferings in him; and this we have hitherto quite rightly left to fate. We should receive admonitions from all sides against the presumption of vying with fate in subjecting poor human creatures to such cruel experiments. And what sort of experiments would they be? Could we, for purposes of prophylaxis, take the responsibility of destroying a satisfactory marriage, or causing a patient to give up a post upon which his livelihood depends? Fortunately, we never find ourselves in the position of having to consider whether such interventions in the patient's real life are justified; we do not possess the plenary powers which they would necessitate, and the subject of our therapeutic experiment would certainly refuse to co-operate in it. In practice, then, such a procedure is virtually excluded; but there are, besides, theoretical objections to it. For the work of analysis proceeds best if the patient's pathogenic experiences belong to the past, so that his ego can stand at a distance from them. In states of acute crisis analysis is to all intents and purposes unusable. The ego's whole interest is taken up by the painful reality and it withholds itself from analysis, which is attempting to go below the surface and uncover the influences of the past. To create a fresh conflict would thus only be to make the work of analysis longer and more difficult.

It will be objected that these remarks are quite unnecessary. Nobody thinks of purposely conjuring up new situations of suffering in order to make it possible for a latent instinctual conflict to be treated. This would not be much to boast of as a prophylactic achievement. We know, for instance, that a patient who has recovered from scarlet fever is immune to a return of the same illness; yet it never occurs to a doctor to take a healthy person who may possibly fall ill of scarlet fever and infect him with scarlet fever in order to make him immune to it. The protective measure must not produce the same situation of danger as is produced by the illness itself, but only something very much slighter, as is the case with vaccination against small-pox and many other similar procedures. In analytic prophylaxis against instinctual conflicts, therefore, the only methods which come into consideration are the other two which we have mentioned: the artificial production of new conflicts in the transference (conflicts which, after all, lack the character of reality), and the arousing of such conflicts in the patient's imagination by talking to him about them and making him familiar with their possibility.

I do not know whether we can assert that the first of these two milder procedures is altogether ruled out in analysis. No experiments have been particularly made in this direction. But difficulties at once suggest themselves, which do not throw a very promising light on such an undertaking. In the first place, the choice of such situations for the transference is very limited. The patients cannot themselves bring all their conflicts into the transference; nor is the analyst able to call out all their possible instinctual conflicts from the transference situation. He may make them jealous or cause them to experience disappointments in love; but no technical purpose is required to bring this about. Such things happen of themselves in any case in most analyses. In the second place, we must not overlook the fact that all measures of this sort would oblige the analyst to behave in an unfriendly way to the patient, and this would have a damaging effect upon the affectionate attitude—upon the positive transference—which is the strongest motive for the patient's taking a share in the joint work of analysis. Thus we should on no account expect very much from this procedure.

This therefore leaves only the one method open to us—the one which was in all probability the only one originally contemplated. We tell the patient about the possibilities of other instinctual conflicts, and we arouse his expectation that such conflicts may occur in him. What we hope is that this information and this warning will have the effect of activating in him one of the conflicts we have indicated, in a modest degree and yet sufficiently for treatment. But this time experience speaks with no uncertain voice. The expected result does not come about. The patient hears our message, but there is no response. He may think to himself: 'This is very interesting, but I feel no trace of it.' We have increased his knowledge, but altered nothing else in him. The situation is much the same as when people read psycho-analytic writings. The reader is 'stimulated' only by those passages which he feels apply to himself—that is, which concern conflicts that are active in him at the time. Everything else leaves him cold. We can have analogous experiences, I think, when we give children sexual enlightenment. I am far from maintaining that this is a harmful or unnecessary thing to do, but it is clear that the prophylactic effect of this liberal measure has been greatly over-estimated. After such enlightenment, children know something they did not know before, but they make no use of the new knowledge that has been presented to them. We come to see that they are not even in so great a hurry to sacrifice for this new knowledge the sexual theories which might be described as a natural growth and which they have constructed in harmony with, and dependence on, their imperfect libidinal organization—theories about the part played by the stork, about the nature of sexual intercourse and about the way in which babies are made. For a long time after they have been given sexual enlightenment they behave like primitive races who have had Christianity thrust upon them and who continue to worship their old idols in secret.[1]

V

We started from the question of how we can shorten the inconveniently long duration of analytic treatment, and, still with this question of time in mind, we went on to consider whether it is possible to achieve a permanent cure or even to prevent future illness by prophylactic treatment. In doing so, we found that the factors which were decisive for the success of our therapeutic efforts were the influence of traumatic aetiology, the relative strength of the instincts which have to be controlled, and something which we have called an alteration of the ego. [See p. 224 above.] Only the second of these factors has been discussed by us in any detail, and in connection with it we have had occasion to recognize the paramount importance of the quantitative factor and to stress the claim of the meta-psychological line of approach to be taken into account in any attempt at explanation.

Concerning the third factor, the alteration of the ego, we have as yet said nothing. When we turn our attention to it, the first impression we receive is that there is much to ask and much to answer here, and that what we have to say about it will prove to be very inadequate. This first impression is confirmed when

---

[1] [These reflections of Freud's on the sexual enlightenment of children may be compared with the less sophisticated ones in his early paper on the subject (1907c).]

we go further into the problem. As is well known, the analytic situation consists in our allying ourselves with the ego of the person under treatment, in order to subdue portions of his id which are uncontrolled—that is to say to include them in the synthesis of his ego. The fact that a co-operation of this kind habitually fails in the case of psychotics affords us a first solid footing for our judgement. The ego, if we are to be able to make such a pact with it, must be a normal one. But a normal ego of this sort is, like normality in general, an ideal fiction. The abnormal ego, which is unserviceable for our purposes, is unfortunately no fiction. Every normal person, in fact, is only normal on the average. His ego approximates to that of the psychotic in some part or other and to a greater or lesser extent; and the degree of its remoteness from one end of the series and of its proximity to the other will furnish us with a provisional measure of what we have so indefinitely termed an 'alteration of the ego'.

If we ask what is the source of the great variety of kinds and degrees of alteration of the ego, we cannot escape the first obvious alternative, that such alterations are either congenital or acquired. Of these, the second sort will be the easier to treat. If they are acquired, it will certainly have been in the course of development, starting from the first years of life. For the ego has to try from the very outset to fulfil its task of mediating between its id and the external world in the service of the pleasure principle, and to protect the id from the dangers of the external world. If, in the course of these efforts, the ego learns to adopt a defensive attitude towards its own id as well and to treat the latter's instinctual demands as external dangers, this happens, at any rate in part, because it understands that a satisfaction of instinct would lead to conflicts with the external world. Thereafter, under the influence of education, the ego grows accustomed to removing the scene of the fight from outside to within and to mastering the *internal* danger before it has become an *external* one; and probably it is most often right in doing so. During this fight on two fronts—later there will be a third front as well[1]—the ego makes use of various procedures for fulfilling its task, which, to put it in general terms, is to avoid danger, anxiety and unpleasure. We call these procedures '*mechanisms of defence*'. Our knowledge of them is not yet

[1] [An oblique reference to the super-ego.]

sufficiently complete. Anna Freud's book (1936) has given us a first insight into their multiplicity and many-sided significance.

It was from one of those mechanisms, repression, that the study of neurotic processes took its whole start. There was never any doubt that repression was not the only procedure which the ego could employ for its purposes. Nevertheless, repression is something quite peculiar and is more sharply differentiated from the other mechanisms than they are from one another. I should like to make this relation to the other mechanisms clear by an analogy, though I know that in these matters analogies never carry us very far. Let us imagine what might have happened to a book, at a time when books were not printed in editions but were written out individually. We will suppose that a book of this kind contained statements which in later times were regarded as undesirable—as, for instance, according to Robert Eisler (1929), the writings of Flavius Josephus must have contained passages about Jesus Christ which were offensive to later Christendom. At the present day, the only defensive mechanism to which the official censorship could resort would be to confiscate and destroy every copy of the whole edition. At that time, however, various methods were used for making the book innocuous. One way would be for the offending passages to be thickly crossed through so that they were illegible. In that case they could not be transcribed, and the next copyist of the book would produce a text which was unexceptionable but which had gaps in certain passages, and so might be un-intelligible in them. Another way, however, if the authorities were not satisfied with this, but wanted also to conceal any indication that the text had been mutilated, would be for them to proceed to distort the text. Single words would be left out or replaced by others, and new sentences interpolated. Best of all, the whole passage would be erased and a new one which said exactly the opposite put in its place. The next transcriber could then produce a text that aroused no suspicion but which was falsified. It no longer contained what the author wanted to say; and it is highly probable that the corrections had not been made in the direction of truth.

If the analogy is not pursued too strictly, we may say that repression has the same relation to the other methods of defence as omission has to distortion of the text, and we may discover in the different forms of this falsification parallels to the variety of ways in which the ego is altered. An attempt may be made to raise the objection that the analogy goes wrong in an essential point, for the distortion of a text is the work of a tendentious censorship, no counterpart to which is to be found in the development of the ego. But this is not so; for a tendentious purpose of this kind is to a great extent represented by the compelling force of the pleasure principle. The psychical apparatus is intolerant of unpleasure; it has to fend it off at all costs, and if the perception of reality entails unpleasure, that perception—that is, the truth—must be sacrificed. Where external dangers are concerned, the individual can help himself for some time by flight and by avoiding the situation of danger, until he is strong enough later on to remove the threat by actively altering reality. But one cannot flee from oneself; flight is no help against internal dangers. And for that reason the defensive mechanisms of the ego are condemned to falsify one's internal perception and to give one only an imperfect and distorted picture of one's id. In its relations to the id, therefore, the ego is paralysed by its restrictions or blinded by its errors; and the result of this in the sphere of psychical events can only be compared to being out walking in a country one does not know and without having a good pair of legs.

The mechanisms of defence serve the purpose of keeping off dangers. It cannot be disputed that they are successful in this; and it is doubtful whether the ego could do without them altogether during its development. But it is also certain that they may become dangers themselves. It sometimes turns out that the ego has paid too high a price for the services they render it. The dynamic expenditure necessary for maintaining them, and the restrictions of the ego which they almost invariably entail, prove a heavy burden on the psychical economy. Moreover, these mechanisms are not relinquished after they have assisted the ego during the difficult years of its development. No one individual, of course, makes use of all the possible mechanisms of defence. Each person uses no more than a selection of them. But these become fixated in his ego. They become regular modes of reaction of his character, which are repeated throughout his life whenever a situation occurs that is similar to the original one. This turns them into infantilisms, and they share the fate of so many institutions which attempt to keep themselves in existence after the time of their usefulness

24

has passed. 'Vernunft wird Unsinn, Wohltat Plage' as the poet complains.[1] The adult's ego, with its increased strength, continues to defend itself against dangers which no longer exist in reality; indeed, it finds itself compelled to seek out those situations in reality which can serve as an approximate substitute for the original danger, so as to be able to justify, in relation to them, its maintaining its habitual modes of reaction. Thus we can easily understand how the defensive mechanisms, by bringing about an ever more extensive alienation from the external world and a permanent weakening of the ego, pave the way for, and encourage, the outbreak of neurosis.

At the moment, however, we are not concerned with the pathogenic role of the defensive mechanisms. What we are trying to discover is what influence the alteration of the ego which corresponds to them has upon our therapeutic efforts. The material for an answer to this question is given in the volume by Anna Freud to which I have already referred. The essential point is that the patient repeats these modes of reaction during the work of analysis as well, that he produces them before our eyes, as it were. In fact, it is only in this way that we get to know them. This does not mean that they make analysis impossible. On the contrary, they constitute half of our analytic task. The other half, the one which was first tackled by analysis in its early days, is the uncovering of what is hidden in the id. During the treatment our therapeutic work is constantly swinging backwards and forwards like a pendulum between a piece of id-analysis and a piece of ego-analysis. In the one case we want to make something from the id conscious, in the other we want to correct something in the ego. The crux of the matter is that the defensive mechanisms directed against former danger recur in the treatment as *resistances* against recovery. It follows from this that the ego treats recovery itself as a new danger.

The therapeutic effect depends on making conscious what is repressed, in the widest sense of the word, in the id. We prepare the way for this making conscious by interpretations and constructions,[2] but we have interpreted only for ourselves not for the patient so long as the ego holds on to its earlier defences and does not give up its resistances. Now these resistances, although

[1] ['Reason becomes unreason, kindness torment.' Goethe, *Faust*, Part I, Scene 4.]
[2] [Cf. the paper on this subject (1937*d*), p. 255 below.]

they belong to the ego, are nevertheless unconscious and in some sense separated off within the ego. The analyst recognizes them more easily than he does the hidden material in the id. One might suppose that it would be sufficient to treat them like portions of the id and, by making them conscious, bring them into connection with the rest of the ego. In this way, we should suppose, one half of the task of analysis would be accomplished; we should not reckon on meeting with a resistance against the uncovering of resistances. But what happens is this. During the work on the resistances the ego withdraws—with a greater or less degree of seriousness—from the agreement on which the analytic situation is founded. The ego ceases to support our efforts at uncovering the id; it opposes them, disobeys the fundamental rule of analysis, and allows no further derivatives of the repressed to emerge. We cannot expect the patient to have a strong conviction of the curative power of analysis. He may have brought along with him a certain amount of confidence in his analyst, which will be strengthened to an effective point by the factors of the positive transference which will be aroused in him. Under the influence of the unpleasurable impulses which he feels as a result of the fresh activation of his defensive conflicts, negative transferences may now gain the upper hand and completely annul the analytic situation. The patient now regards the analyst as no more than a stranger who is making disagreeable demands on him, and he behaves towards him exactly like a child who does not like the stranger and does not believe anything he says. If the analyst tries to explain to the patient one of the distortions made by him for the purposes of defence, and to correct it, he finds him uncomprehending and inaccessible to sound arguments. Thus we see that there *is* a resistance against the uncovering of resistances, and the defensive mechanisms really do deserve the name which we gave them originally, before they had been more closely examined. They are resistances not only to the making conscious of contents of the id, but also to the analysis as a whole, and thus to recovery.

The effect brought about in the ego by the defences can rightly be described as an 'alteration of the ego' if by that we understand a deviation from the fiction of a normal ego which would guarantee unshakable loyalty to the work of analysis. It is easy, then, to accept the fact, shown by daily experience, that the outcome of an analytic treatment depends essentially on the strength and on the depth of root of these resistances that bring about an alteration of the ego, Once again we are confronted with the importance of the quantitative factor, and once again we are reminded that analysis can only draw upon definite and limited amounts of energy which have to be measured against the hostile forces. And it seems as if victory is in fact as a rule on the side of the big battalions.

VI

The next question we come to is whether every alteration of the ego—in our sense of the term—is acquired during the defensive struggles of the earliest years. There can be no doubt about the answer. We have no reason to dispute the existence and importance of original, innate distinguishing characteristics of the ego. This is made certain by the single fact that each person makes a selection from the possible mechanisms of defence, that he always uses a few only of them and always the same ones [p. 237 above]. This would seem to indicate that each ego is endowed from the first with individual dispositions and trends, though it is true that we cannot specify their nature or what determines them. Moreover, we know that we must not exaggerate the difference between inherited and acquired characters into an antithesis; what was acquired by our forefathers certainly forms an important part of what we inherit. When we speak of an 'archaic heritage' [1] we are usually thinking only of the id and we seem to assume that at the beginning of the individual's life no ego is as yet in existence. But we shall not overlook the fact that id and ego are originally one; nor does it imply any mystical overvaluation of heredity if we think it credible that, even before the ego has come into existence, the lines of development, trends and reactions which it will later exhibit are already laid down for it. The psychological peculiarities of families, races and nations, even in their attitude to analysis, allow of no other explanation. Indeed, more than this: analytic experience has forced on us a conviction that even particular psychical contents, such as symbolism, have no other sources than hereditary transmission, and researches in various

[1] [See an Editor's Note to Part I of the Third Essay in *Moses and Monotheism* (1939a), p. 102 above.]

fields of social anthropology, make it plausible to suppose that other, equally specialized precipitates left by early human development are also present in the archaic heritage.

With the recognition that the properties of the ego which we meet with in the form of resistances can equally well be determined by heredity as acquired in defensive struggles, the topographical distinction between what is ego and what is id loses much of its value for our investigation. If we advance a step further in our analytic experience, we come upon resistances of another kind, which we can no longer localize and which seem to depend on fundamental conditions in the mental apparatus. I can only give a few examples of this type of resistance; the whole field of enquiry is still bewilderingly strange and insufficiently explored. We come across people, for instance, to whom we should be inclined to attribute a special 'adhesiveness of the libido'.[1] The processes which the treatment sets in motion in them are so much slower than in other people because, apparently, they cannot make up their minds to detach libidinal cathexes from one object and displace them on to another, although we can discover no special reason for this cathectic loyalty. One meets with the opposite type of person, too, in whom the libido seems particularly mobile; it enters readily upon the new cathexes suggested by analysis, abandoning its former ones in exchange for them. The difference between the two types is comparable to the one felt by a sculptor, according to whether he works in hard stone or soft clay. Unfortunately, in this second type the results of analysis often turn out to be very impermanent: the new cathexes are soon given up once more, and we have an impression, not of having worked in clay, but of having written on water. In the words of the proverb: 'Soon got, soon gone.'[2]

In another group of cases we are surprised by an attitude in our patients which can only be put down to a depletion of the plasticity, the capacity for change and further development, which we should ordinarily expect. We are, it is true, prepared

[1] [The term occurs in Lecture XXII of the *Introductory Lectures* (1916–17), *Standard Ed.*, 16, 348. This characteristic and the more generalized 'psychical inertia' discussed below are not always treated separately in Freud's earlier writings. A list of a number of passages in which the topics are touched upon is given in an Editor's footnote to 'A Case of Paranoia' (1915*f*), *Standard Ed.*, 14, 272.]

[2] ['*Wie gewonnen, so zerronnen.*']

to find in analysis a certain amount of psychical inertia.[1] When the work of analysis has opened up new paths for an instinctual impulse, we almost invariably observe that the impulse does not enter upon them without marked hesitation. We have called this behaviour, perhaps not quite correctly, 'resistance from the id'.[2] But with the patients I here have in mind, all the mental processes, relationships and distributions of force are unchangeable, fixed and rigid. One finds the same thing in very old people, in which case it is explained as being due to what is described as force of habit or an exhaustion of receptivity—a kind of psychical entropy.[3] But we are dealing here with people who are still young. Our theoretical knowledge does not seem adequate to give a correct explanation of such types. Probably some temporal characteristics are concerned—some alterations of a rhythm of development in psychical life which we have not yet appreciated.

In yet another group of cases the distinguishing characteristics of the ego, which are to be held responsible as sources of resistance against analytic treatment and as impediments to therapeutic success, may spring from different and deeper roots. Here we are dealing with the ultimate things which psychological research can learn about: the behaviour of the two primal instincts, their distribution, mingling and defusion—things which we cannot think of as being confined to a single province of the mental apparatus, the id, the ego or the super-ego. No stronger impression arises from the resistances during the work of analysis than of there being a force which is defending itself by every possible means against recovery and which is absolutely resolved to hold on to illness and suffering. One portion of this force has been recognized by us, undoubtedly with justice, as the sense of guilt and need for punishment, and has been localized by us in the ego's relation to the super-ego. But this is only the portion of it which is, as it were, psychically bound by the super-ego and thus becomes recognizable; other quotas of the same force, whether bound or free,

---

[1] [See footnote 1 on last page.]

[2] [See Addendum A (a) to Inhibitions, Symptoms and Anxiety (1926d), Standard Ed., 20, 160.]

[3] [The same analogy occurs in a passage in the 'Wolf Man' case history (1918b), dealing with this same psychological characteristic. Standard Ed., 17, 116.]

may be at work in other, unspecified places. If we take into consideration the total picture made up of the phenomena of masochism immanent in so many people, the negative therapeutic reaction and the sense of guilt found in so many neurotics, we shall no longer be able to adhere to the belief that mental events are exclusively governed by the desire for pleasure. These phenomena are unmistakable indications of the presence of a power in mental life which we call the instinct of aggression or of destruction according to its aims, and which we trace back to the original death instinct of living matter. It is not a question of an antithesis between an optimistic and a pessimistic theory of life. Only by the concurrent or mutually opposing action[1] of the two primal instincts—Eros and the death-instinct—, never by one or the other alone, can we explain the rich multiplicity of the phenomena of life.

How parts of these two classes of instincts combine to fulfil the various vital functions, under what conditions such combinations grow looser or break up, to what disturbances these changes correspond and with what feelings the perceptual scale of the pleasure principle replies to them—these are problems whose elucidation would be the most rewarding achievement of psychological research. For the moment we must bow to the superiority of the forces against which we see our efforts come to nothing. Even to exert a psychical influence on simple masochism is a severe tax upon our powers.

In studying the phenomena which testify to the activity of the destructive instinct, we are not confined to observations on pathological material. Numerous facts of normal mental life call for an explanation of this kind, and the sharper our eye grows, the more copiously they strike us. The subject is too new and too important for me to treat it as a side-issue in this discussion. I shall therefore content myself with selecting a few sample cases.

Here is one instance. It is well known that at all periods there have been, as there still are, people who can take as their sexual objects members of their own sex as well as of the opposite one,

---

[1] [The phrase was a favourite one of Freud's. It will be found, for instance, in the first paragraph of *The Interpretation of Dreams* (1900a), *Standard Ed.*, **4**, 1. His liking for it reflects his loyalty to a 'fundamental dualistic point of view'. Cf. *The Ego and the Id* (1923b), ibid., **19**, 46, and p. 246 below.]

without the one trend interfering with the other. We call such people bisexuals, and we accept their existence without feeling much surprise about it. We have come to learn, however, that every human being is bisexual in this sense and that his libido is distributed, either in a manifest or a latent fashion, over objects of both sexes. But we are struck by the following point. Whereas in the first class of people the two trends have got on together without clashing, in the second and more numerous class they are in a state of irreconcilable conflict. A man's heterosexuality will not put up with any homosexuality, and *vice versa*. If the former is the stronger it succeeds in keeping the latter latent and forcing it away from satisfaction in reality. On the other hand, there is no greater danger for a man's heterosexual function than its being disturbed by his latent homosexuality. We might attempt to explain this by saying that each individual only has a certain quota of libido at his disposal, for which the two rival trends have to struggle. But it is not clear why the rivals do not always divide up the available quota of libido between them according to their relative strength, since they are able to do so in a number of cases. We are forced to the conclusion that the tendency to a conflict is something special, something which is newly added to the situation, irrespective of the quantity of libido. An independently-emerging tendency to conflict of this sort can scarcely be attributed to anything but the intervention of an element of free aggressiveness.

If we recognize the case we are discussing as an expression of the destructive or aggressive instinct, the question at once arises whether this view should not be extended to other instances of conflict, and, indeed, whether all that we know about psychical conflict should not be revised from this new angle. After all, we assume that in the course of man's development from a primitive state to a civilized one his aggressiveness undergoes a very considerable degree of internalization or turning inwards; if so, his internal conflicts would certainly be the proper equivalent for the external struggles which have then ceased. I am well aware that the dualistic theory according to which an instinct of death or of destruction or aggression claims equal rights as a partner with Eros as manifested in the libido, has found little sympathy and has not really been accepted even among psycho-analysts. This made me all the more pleased when not long ago I came upon this theory of mine in the writings of one of the

great thinkers of ancient Greece. I am very ready to give up the
prestige of originality for the sake of such a confirmation,
especially as I can never be certain, in view of the wide extent
of my reading in early years, whether what I took for a new
creation might not be an effect of cryptomnesia.[1]

Empedocles of Acragas (Girgenti),[2] born about 495 B.C., is
one of the grandest and most remarkable figures in the history
of Greek civilization. The activities of his many-sided personality pursued the most varied directions. He was an investigator
and a thinker, a prophet and a magician, a politician, a phil-
anthropist and a physician with a knowledge of natural science.
He was said to have freed the town of Selinunte from malaria,
and his contemporaries revered him as a god. His mind seems
to have united the sharpest contrasts. He was exact and sober
in his physical and physiological researches, yet he did not
shrink from the obscurities of mysticism, and built up cosmic
speculations of astonishingly imaginative boldness. Capelle
compares him with Dr. Faust 'to whom many a secret was
revealed'.[3] Born as he was at a time when the realm of science
was not yet divided into so many provinces, some of his theories
must inevitably strike us as primitive. He explained the variety
of things by the mixture of the four elements, earth, air, fire
and water. He held that all nature was animate, and he
believed in the transmigration of souls. But he also included in
his theoretical body of knowledge such modern ideas as the
gradual evolution of living creatures, the survival of the fittest
and a recognition of the part played by chance ($\tau\acute{\nu}\chi\eta$) in that
evolution.

But the theory of Empedocles which especially deserves our
interest is one which approximates so closely to the psychoanalytic theory of the instincts that we should be tempted to
maintain that the two are identical, if it were not for the difference that the Greek philosopher's theory is a cosmic phantasy
while ours is content to claim biological validity. At the same
time, the fact that Empedocles ascribes to the universe the same

[1] [Cf. some remarks on this subject in a paper by Freud on Josef
Popper-Lynkeus (1923*f*), *Standard Ed.*, **19**, 261 and 263 *n*.]
[2] I have based what follows on a work by Wilhelm Capelle (1935).
[The Sicilian town is more commonly known as Agrigentum.]
[3] ['*Dem gar manch Geheimnis wurde kund.*' Modified from a line in
Faust's first speech. (Goethe, *Faust*, Part I, Scene 1.)]

animate nature as to individual organisms robs this difference
of much of its importance.

The philosopher taught that two principles governed events
in the life of the universe and in the life of the mind, and that
those principles were everlastingly at war with each other. He
called them φιλία (love) and νεῖκος (strife). Of these two
powers—which he conceived of as being at bottom 'natural
forces operating like instincts, and by no means intelligences
with a conscious purpose' [1]—the one strives to agglomerate the
primal particles of the four elements into a single unity, while
the other, on the contrary, seeks to undo all those fusions and to
separate the primal particles of the elements from one another.
Empedocles thought of the process of the universe as a continuous, never-ceasing alternation of periods, in which the one
or the other of the two fundamental forces gain the upper hand,
so that at one time love and at another strife puts its purpose
completely into effect and dominates the universe, after which
the other, vanquished, side asserts itself and in its turn defeats
its partner.

The two fundamental principles of Empedocles—φιλία and
νεῖκος—are, both in name and function, the same as our two
primal instincts, *Eros* and *destructiveness*, the first of which
endeavours to combine what exists into ever greater unities,
while the second endeavours to dissolve those combinations and
to destroy the structures to which they have given rise. We
shall not be surprised, however, to find that, on its re-emergence
after two and a half millennia, this theory has been altered in
some of its features. Apart from the restriction to the biophysical
field which is imposed on us, we no longer have as our basic
substances the four elements of Empedocles; what is living has
been sharply differentiated from what is inanimate, and we no
longer think of the mingling and separation of particles of sub-
stance, but of the soldering together and defusion of instinctual
components. Moreover, we have provided some sort of biological basis for the principle of 'strife' by tracing back our
instinct of destruction to the death instinct, to the urge of what
is living to return to an inanimate state. This is not to deny that
an analogous instinct [2] already existed earlier, nor, of course, to
assert that an instinct of this sort only came into existence with

[1] Capelle (1935), 186.
[2] [I.e. analogous to the death instinct.]

the emergence of life. And no one can foresee in what guise the nucleus of truth contained in the theory of Empedocles will present itself to later understanding.[1]

VII

In 1927, Ferenczi read an instructive paper on the problem of the termination of analyses.[2] It ends with a comforting assurance that 'analysis is not an endless process, but one which can be brought to a natural end with sufficient skill and patience on the analyst's part'.[3] The paper as a whole, however, seems to me to be in the nature of a warning not to aim at shortening analysis but at deepening it. Ferenczi makes the further important point that success depends very largely on the analyst's having learnt sufficiently from his own 'errors and mistakes' and having got the better of 'the weak points in his own personality'.[4] This provides an important supplement to our theme. Among the factors which influence the prospects of analytic treatment and add to its difficulties in the same manner as the resistances, must be reckoned not only the nature of the patient's ego but the individuality of the analyst.

It cannot be disputed that analysts in their own personalities have not invariably come up to the standard of psychical normality to which they wish to educate their patients. Opponents of analysis often point to this fact with scorn and use it as an argument to show the uselessness of analytic exertions. We might reject this criticism as making unjustifiable demands. Analysts are people who have learned to practise a particular art; alongside of this, they may be allowed to be human beings like anyone else. After all, nobody maintains that a physician is incapable of treating internal diseases if his own internal organs are not sound; on the contrary, it may be argued that

[1] [Empedocles was mentioned once more by Freud in a footnote to Chapter II of his posthumous *Outline of Psycho-Analysis* (1940a [1938]), p. 149 above.—Freud made some further remarks on the destructive instinct in a letter written shortly after this paper to Princess Marie Bonaparte. An extract from it appears in the Editor's Introduction to *Civilization and its Discontents* (1930a), *Standard Ed.*, **21**, 63.]

[2] [This was a paper read at the Innsbruck Psycho-Analytical Congress in 1927. It was published in the following year.]

[3] [Ferenczi, 1928; English trans., 1955, 86.]

[4] [Ferenczi, loc. cit.]

there are certain advantages in a man who is himself threatened with tuberculosis specializing in the treatment of persons suffering from that disease. But the cases are not on all fours. So long as he is capable of practising at all, a doctor suffering from disease of the lungs or heart is not handicapped either in diagnosing or treating internal complaints; whereas the special conditions of analytic work do actually cause the analyst's own defects to interfere with his making a correct assessment of the state of things in his patient and reacting to them in a useful way. It is therefore reasonable to expect of an analyst, as a part of his qualifications, a considerable degree of mental normality and correctness. In addition, he must possess some kind of superiority, so that in certain analytic situations he can act as a model for his patient and in others as a teacher. And finally we must not forget that the analytic relationship is based on a love of truth—that is, on a recognition of reality—and that it precludes any kind of sham or deceit.

Here let us pause for a moment to assure the analyst that he has our sincere sympathy in the very exacting demands he has to fulfil in carrying out his activities. It almost looks as if analysis were the third of those 'impossible' professions in which one can be sure beforehand of achieving unsatisfying results. The other two, which have been known much longer, are education and government.[1] Obviously we cannot demand that the prospective analyst should be a perfect being before he takes up analysis, in other words that only persons of such high and rare perfection should enter the profession. But where and how is the poor wretch to acquire the ideal qualifications which he will need in his profession? The answer is, in an analysis of himself, with which his preparation for his future activity begins. For practical reasons this analysis can only be short and incomplete. Its main object is to enable his teacher to make a judgement as to whether the candidate can be accepted for further training. It has accomplished its purpose if it gives the learner a firm conviction of the existence of the unconscious, if it enables him, when repressed material emerges, to perceive in himself things which would otherwise be incredible to him, and if it shows him a first sample of the technique which has proved to be the only effective one in analytic work. This alone

---

[1] [Cf. a similar passage in Freud's review of Aichhorn's *Wayward Youth* (Freud, 1925*f*), *Standard Ed.*, **19**, 273.]

would not suffice for his instruction; but we reckon on the stimuli that he has received in his own analysis not ceasing when it ends and on the processes of remodelling the ego continuing spontaneously in the analysed subject and making use of all subsequent experiences in this newly-acquired sense. This does in fact happen, and in so far as it happens it makes the analysed subject qualified to be an analyst himself.

Unfortunately something else happens as well. In trying to describe this, one can only rely on impressions. Hostility on the one side and partisanship on the other create an atmosphere which is not favourable to objective investigation. It seems that a number of analysts learn to make use of defensive mechanisms which allow them to divert the implications and demands of analysis from themselves (probably by directing them on to other people), so that they themselves remain as they are and are able to withdraw from the critical and corrective influence of analysis. Such an event may justify the words of the writer who warns us that when a man is endowed with power it is hard for him not to misuse it.[1] Sometimes, when we try to understand this, we are driven into drawing a disagreeable analogy with the effect of X-rays on people who handle them without taking special precautions. It would not be surprising if the effect of a constant preoccupation with all the repressed material which struggles for freedom in the human mind were to stir up in the analyst as well all the instinctual demands which he is otherwise able to keep under suppression. These, too, are 'dangers of analysis', though they threaten, not the passive but the active partner in the analytic situation; and we ought not to neglect to meet them. There can be no doubt how this is to be done. Every analyst should periodically—at intervals of five years or so—submit himself to analysis once more, without feeling ashamed of taking this step. This would mean, then, that not only the therapeutic analysis of patients but his own analysis would change from a terminable into an interminable task.

At this point, however, we must guard against a misconception. I am not intending to assert that analysis is altogether an endless business. Whatever one's theoretical attitude to the question may be, the termination of an analysis is, I think a practical matter. Every experienced analyst will be able to

[1] Anatole France, *La révolte des anges.*

recall a number of cases in which he has bidden his patient a permanent farewell *rebus bene gestis*.[1] In cases of what is known as character-analysis there is a far smaller discrepancy between theory and practice. Here it is not easy to foresee a natural end, even if one avoids any exaggerated expectations and sets the analysis no excessive tasks. Our aim will not be to rub off every peculiarity of human character for the sake of a schematic 'normality', nor yet to demand that the person who has been 'thoroughly analysed' shall feel no passions and develop no internal conflicts. The business of the analysis is to secure the best possible psychological conditions for the functions of the ego; with that it has discharged its task.

VIII

Both in therapeutic and in character-analyses we notice that two themes come into especial prominence and give the analyst an unusual amount of trouble. It soon becomes evident that a general principle is at work here. The two themes are tied to the distinction between the sexes; one is as characteristic of males as the other is of females. In spite of the dissimilarity of their content, there is an obvious correspondence between them. Something which both sexes have in common has been forced, by the difference between the sexes, into different forms of expression.

The two corresponding themes are in the female, an *envy for the penis*—a positive striving to possess a male genital—and, in the male, a struggle against his passive or feminine attitude to another male. What is common to the two themes was singled out at an early date by psycho-analytic nomenclature as an attitude towards the castration complex. Subsequently Alfred Adler brought the term 'masculine protest' into current use. It fits the case of males perfectly; but I think that, from the start, 'repudiation of femininity' would have been the correct description of this remarkable feature in the psychical life of human beings.

In trying to introduce this factor into the structure of our theory, we must not overlook the fact that it cannot, by its very nature, occupy the same position in both sexes. In males the striving to be masculine is completely ego-syntonic from

[1] ['Things having gone well.']

the first; the passive attitude, since it presupposes an acceptance of castration, is energetically repressed, and often its presence is only indicated by excessive overcompensations. In females, too, the striving to be masculine is ego-syntonic at a certain period—namely in the phallic phase, before the development to femininity has set in. But it then succumbs to the momentous process of repression whose outcome, as has so often been shown, determines the fortunes of a woman's femininity.[1] A great deal depends on whether a sufficient amount of her masculinity complex escapes repression and exercises a permanent influence on her character. Normally, large portions of the complex are transformed and contribute to the construction of her femininity: the appeased wish for a penis is destined to be converted into a wish for a baby and for a husband, who possesses a penis. It is strange, however, how often we find that the wish for masculinity has been retained in the unconscious and, from out of its state of repression, exercises a disturbing influence.

As will be seen from what I have said, in both cases it is the attitude proper to the opposite sex which has succumbed to repression. I have already stated elsewhere[2] that it was Wilhelm Fliess who called my attention to this point. Fliess was inclined to regard the antithesis between the sexes as the true cause and primal motive force of repression. I am only repeating what I said then in disagreeing with his view, when I decline to sexualize repression in this way—that is, to explain it on biological grounds instead of on purely psychological ones.

The paramount importance of these two themes—in females the wish for a penis and in males the struggle against passivity —did not escape Ferenczi's notice. In the paper read by him in 1927 he made it a requirement that in every successful analysis those two complexes must have been mastered.[3] I

[1] [Cf., for instance, 'Female Sexuality' (1931*b*), *Standard Ed.*, 21, 229 f.]

[2] ' "A Child is being Beaten" ' (1919*e*), *Standard Ed.*, 17, 200 ff. [Actually Fliess is not mentioned by name in that paper.]

[3] '. . . Every male patient must attain a feeling of equality in relation to the physician as a sign that he has overcome his fear of castration; every female patient, if her neurosis is to be regarded as fully disposed of, must have got rid of her masculinity complex and must emotionally accept without a trace of resentment the implications of her female role.' (Ferenczi, 1928, 8 [English trans., 84].)

should like to add that, speaking from my own experience, I think that in this Ferenczi was asking a very great deal. At no other point in one's analytic work does one suffer more from an oppressive feeling that all one's repeated efforts have been in vain, and from a suspicion that one has been 'preaching to the winds', than when one is trying to persuade a woman to abandon her wish for a penis on the ground of its being un-realizable or when one is seeking to convince a man that a passive attitude to men does not always signify castration and that it is indispensable in many relationships in life. The rebellious overcompensation of the male produces one of the strongest transference-resistances. He refuses to subject him-self to a father-substitute, or to feel indebted to him for any-thing, and consequently he refuses to accept his recovery from the doctor. No analogous transference can arise from the female's wish for a penis, but it is the source of outbreaks of severe depression in her, owing to an internal conviction that the analysis will be of no use and that nothing can be done to help her. And we can only agree that she is right, when we learn that her strongest motive in coming for treatment was the hope that, after all, she might still obtain a male organ, the lack of which was so painful to her.

But we also learn from this that it is not important in what form the resistance appears, whether as a transference or not. The decisive thing remains that the resistance prevents any change from taking place—that everything stays as it was. We often have the impression that with the wish for a penis and the masculine protest we have penetrated through all the psy-chological strata and have reached bedrock, and that thus our activities are at an end. This is probably true, since, for the psychical field, the biological field does in fact play the part of the underlying bedrock. The repudiation of femininity can be nothing else than a biological fact, a part of the great riddle of sex.[1] It would be hard to say whether and when we have

[1] We must not be misled by the term 'masculine protest' into sup-posing that what the man is repudiating is his passive attitude [as such] —what might be called the social aspect of femininity. Such a view is contradicted by an observation that is easily verifiable—namely that such men often display a masochistic attitude—a state that amounts to bondage—towards women. What they reject is not passivity in general, but passivity towards a male. In other words, the 'masculine protest' is

succeeded in mastering this factor in an analytic treatment. We can only console ourselves with the certainty that we have given the person analysed every possible encouragement to re-examine and alter his attitude to it.

in fact nothing else than castration anxiety. [The state of sexual 'bondage' in men had been alluded to by Freud in his paper on 'The Taboo of Virginity' (1918a), *Standard Ed.*, **11**, 194.]

PART TWO

Discussion of "Analysis Terminable and Interminable"

A New Look at Freud's "Analysis Terminable and Interminable"

JACOB A. ARLOW

It would be difficult to imagine a psychoanalytic experience more stimulating or thought-provoking than rereading Freud's "Analysis Terminable and Interminable" and examining from our current perspective the many important issues it raises. The questions Freud posed then are fundamental to controversies in psychoanalysis to this very day. Some of the answers he proposed seem outdated and patently incorrect, while others are penetratingly perceptive, anticipating major lines of development for psychoanalytic technique.

It should be recalled that, only a few years before he wrote this paper, Freud had revised his concept of the psychic apparatus in a radical way. He had ceased trying to understand mental phenomena from a predominantly topographic point of view in favor of a structural approach, an approach which emphasized the interplay of persistent, organized forces in the mind. Whereas the topographic model stressed the pathogenic significance of what was repressed into the system *Ucs*, the structural model stressed the role of intrapsychic conflict and compromise formation. Obviously, it was not easy for Freud, at the end of his days, to make a clean and decisive break with a model of conceptualization which for so many years he had found so fruitful. In *The Ego and the Id* (1923), for example, he stated that henceforth he would be using the terms *conscious* and *unconscious* in a purely descriptive, rather than systematic, way. Nevertheless, in *An Outline of Psychoanalysis* (1940), he reverted to discussions of the characteristics of the systems *Ucs*, *Pcs*, and *Pcpt-Cs*. On reexamining "Analysis Terminable and Interminable," it is both interesting and instructive to observe how concepts from the two different frames of reference are used side by side, sometimes in a contradictory fashion.

In essence "Analysis Terminable and Interminable" is an essay on psychoanalytic technique. Freud asks: How can we make the process of analysis shorter? How can we make it more effective? Should we be able to protect the analysand against recurrence of his or her illness? Would it be possible to make an analysand immune to psychological illness in general? Obviously, before these questions can be addressed, one must confront the issue of the nature of the pathological process. The rationale of any technique clearly must relate to how it goes about correcting the pathological process and its effects. It is at this point that the conceptual model becomes important. In the topographic theory, the system *Ucs* is the great reservoir or container of the instinctual drives. According to this theory, when discharge of the instinctual drives is blocked by repression, psychological illness supervenes. We can recognize in this formulation the lingering effects of an "actual" theory of pathogenesis. The implications for technique follow quite logically. The goal of technique becomes one of overcoming repression. Its tangible result is the recollection of an event that had been forgotten.

Freud states this quite explicitly. In discussing the possibility of a person becoming "completely analysed," Freud says, "It is as though it were possible by means of analysis to attain to a level of absolute psychical normality—a level, moreover, which we could feel confident would be able to remain stable, *as though, perhaps, we had succeeded in resolving every one of the patient's repressions and in filling in all the gaps in his memory*" (pp. 219–20, emphasis added). Elsewhere, Freud says, "Thus the real achievement of analytic therapy would be the subsequent correction of the original process of repression, a correction which puts an end to the dominance of the quantitative factor" (p. 227). In actual practice, as Freud noted in "Constructions in Analysis" (1937), this hardly ever happens, and it becomes necessary to conjecture, or to "reconstruct" missing links in the personal history. Several authors (Esman 1973, Arlow 1978, Blum 1979) have noted that patients who have had long and repeated exposure to the primal scene, for example, do not recover the memory, even after convincing reconstruction and excellent therapeutic results. In other words, undoing repression, as exemplified by the recollection of forgotten memories, is not in itself the *summum bonum* of psychoanalytic technique.

In concentrating on undoing repression during therapy, Freud reached certain conclusions about the role of the defense mechanisms that in many respects run counter to our current views. He says, "The adult's ego, with its increased strength, continues to defend itself against dangers which no longer exist in reality; indeed, it finds itself compelled to seek out those situations in reality which can serve as an approximate substitute for the original danger, so as to be able to justify, in relation to them, its maintaining its habitual modes of reaction. Thus we can easily understand how the defensive mechanisms, by bringing about an ever more extensive alienation from the external world and a permanent weakening of the ego, pave the way for, and encourage, the outbreak of neurosis" (p. 238). Later in the same section, Freud adds, "The crux of the matter is that the defensive mechanisms directed against former danger recur in the treatment as *resistances* against recovery. It follows from this that the ego treats recovery itself as a new danger" (p. 238, emphasis in the original).

However, it runs counter to the concept of the ego as an agency of adaptation (Hartmann 1939) to posit the ego seeking out new situations as approximate substitutes for an original danger in order to rationalize maintaining pathogenic defense mechanisms. It is much more in keeping with clinical experience to view the situation in the following light: Because of the persistent effect of unconscious fantasy wishes, reality tends to be misperceived, misinterpreted, and "misresponded to" in terms of these unconscious fantasies. Thus, the patient responds to an external situation in terms that would be appropriate in response to his unconscious fantasy. For example, some phobic patients behave as if entering a tunnel were something dangerous to do, because unconsciously they are responding to a fantasy of entering the mother's body, within which a dangerous rival lurks, ready to destroy them. Situations in reality that are in some way comparable to or reminiscent of unconscious fantasies and traumatic incidents tend to evoke and reactivate such fantasies and the conflictual wishes associated with them, and thereby also evoke the need to fend off the dangers connected with those wishes (Arlow 1969). Only from the most superficial, phenomenological point of view can it be said that the ego treats recovery itself as a new danger. In the unconscious portion of the ego, it is the threatened confrontation with the derivatives of the id impulses that signals the need for defensive activity.

These ideas are, of course, Freud's own, subordinated at the time to his emphasis on the importance of recollection in the therapeutic process. In much the same way, Freud referred to transference as a resistance. Insofar as transference substitutes repetition for recollection, this is correct. Transference is a resistance to remembering. At the same time, however, transference does advance the analytic effort. Actually, transference is an example of compromise formation. It is a dynamically determined derivative of the unconscious instinctual conflict. Transference allows for a certain amount of instinctual discharge and gratification, but it does so through a process of displacement from the primary object to the analyst, from the past onto the present. Like a symptom, a dream, or a parapraxis, transference is a distorted representation of a persistent, conflictual, unconscious fantasy. The analysis of the transference, like the analysis of defenses, serves the purpose of bringing into clear expression the hierarchically layered derivatives of the unconscious wish.

From the perspective of *structural* theory, the central technical issue resides not in the uncovering of the repressed nor in the pathogenic role of defense mechanisms, but rather in the analysis of the compromise formations the ego has been able to effect (Brenner 1976). Some compromise formations are adaptive and effective; others are ineffective and pathogenic. The issue is the successful or adequate resolution of conflict, rather than the recovery of the repressed memory. The analysis of the id wish and that of the ego defenses are of equal importance during therapy; the latter is not subordinate to the former in significance. Freud's metaphor comparing psychoanalytic technique to the swinging of the pendulum—that is, first one analyses a bit of the id, then one analyses a bit of the ego's defenses—demonstrates the increasing attention he was paying to the role of conflict and to the importance of appropriate compromise formation as the key to improvement. He makes the point, for example, that only when the etiology of the case is "predominantly traumatic" will analysis "succeed in doing what it is so superlatively able to do"; "only then will it, thanks to having strengthened the patient's ego, succeed in *replacing by a correct solution the inadequate decision made in his early life* (p. 220, emphasis added). He says, in effect, that analytic therapy endeavors "to replace repressions that are insecure by reliable ego-syntonic controls," although it does not "always achieve [that] aim to its full extent" (p. 229).

Throughout his discussion of why analysis takes so long and why the results frequently fail to come up to our expectations, Freud repeatedly emphasizes what he calls the quantitative factor—that is to say, the strength of the instinctual drives and the strength of the resistance to ego modification. In both instances, he focuses on the factor of congenital endowment. His description of the defenses advances the idea of primary congenital variations of the ego. He says that every individual selects only certain of the possible defensive mechanisms and invariably employs those which he has selected. Actually, this is not the case. It is true that, in the process of symptom formation, hysterics selectively favor repression, conversion, displacement, and avoidance. Similarly, patients with obsessive-compulsive neurosis preferentially employ isolation, reaction formation, undoing, and rationalization. However, as Brenner (1981) has made clear, in all patients and in all individuals one may observe the use of a wide range of mental mechanisms in the various compromise formations that the ego effects. Nor are these mechanisms utilized exclusively for purposes of defense; they may be employed to facilitate drive gratification or self-punitive tendencies. As a result, Brenner has suggested that it would be more accurate to refer to these psychological phenomena simply as "mental mechanisms," rather than as mechanisms of defense. Furthermore, there is considerable clinical evidence demonstrating how the preferential utilization of a particular mechanism of defense may be the consequence of specific object relations and identifications (Arlow 1952, Hartmann 1953, Wangh 1959), and so constitute an outgrowth of experience, rather than a congenital predisposition.

In trying to explain why analysis so often fails to achieve its therapeutic goals, Freud uses several different levels of theoretical conceptualization. Explanations such as "the stickiness of the libido" or "the amount of free aggression" belong to the realm of metapsychological formulation (Waelder 1962). Other explanations, such as the effect of an unconscious sense of guilt leading to a need for punishment, proceed at the level of clinical theory. It is very difficult to establish the validity of metapsychological interpretations when applied to an individual case. This is not, however, the situation with explanations based on clinical theory. Since the publication of "Analysis Terminable and Interminable" much has been learned about those clinical factors, especially in the transference, that serve to prolong the length of treatment and to undermine its therapeutic effects.

The termination phase in itself frequently represents to the patient the last opportunity to fulfill the repressed unconscious wishes that form part of the hidden agenda with which he entered analysis (Nunberg 1926). Many analysts feel that, of necessity, the termination phase is characterized by a period of mourning, because it represents a recapitulation of the basic transference, which reflects the vicissitudes of childhood separation experiences. While this is often true, it is not always the case. Unresolved instinctual and narcissistic aspirations from all levels of development may quietly frustrate the therapeutic process. There is a class of patients, for example, who enter treatment, usually in their mid- or late thirties, slightly depressed and with vague complaints that do not conform to any readily recognizable syndrome. They may mention in passing that they feel disappointed in themselves for not having attained their full potential or that perhaps there is some hidden gift or talent within them that has to be unblocked by treatment. It frequently turns out that these patients entertain grandiose self-images to which they aspire and that analysis represents to them the last, magical instrument whereby the wish for transformation can be achieved (Reich 1953). If they fail to achieve their goals, they feel it is because the analysis has not gone deep enough or the analyst is not capable. Another one, they believe, might be better.

There are certain other grandiose expectations that some patients have from analysis, which they stubbornly refuse to surrender. It is not just that some women—and men too—wish to acquire the paternal phallus. What they want is the biggest, the grandest, one in the whole world. Nothing less, not even outstanding success in real life, will satisfy them. Sometimes such fantasies bear a specific relationship to the analytic situation. Orens (1955) described a patient who had no inclination to leave treatment, in spite of the fact that she had made excellent progress in overcoming her difficulties. It turned out that the patient really wanted to stay in analysis forever, because, to her, being in analysis was comparable to being pregnant. The analytic chamber constituted the womb and she was the baby/penis contained therein. She had a fantasy of a perpetual pregnancy; unconsciously, so long as she was in analysis she remained phallic.

Schmideberg (1938) has described how analyst and analysand may be guided unconsciously by omnipotent anticipations of how the individual should be at the end of the treatment. The "fully analyzed" person is expected never to have conflicts, to be immune to anxiety, and so forth. Such descriptions, Schmideberg points out, are latter-day articulations of what a child feels it means to be grown-up. This was illustrated to me dramatically by a patient who became depressed when I made a slip of the tongue. If I, a supposedly "fully analysed" person, was not in complete control, how could I ever help her to achieve that goal? It made her think of wetting the bed when she was a child and of how humiliated she had felt at a recent elegant dinner party, where she was asked to pour the tea and, because of a broken spout, the tea ran all over the place.

Mention should also be made of a whole range of specific transference fantasies that are often kept in abeyance for some time and appear either during the termination phase or shortly after the analysis has been ended. The patient may feel some discomfort and return for consultation or treatment due to an unanalysed transference residue, unconsciously sequestered for the end of the analysis. One patient, for example, who was the son of a surgeon, grew up as the only Jew in a small New England town and had been teased and made to feel humiliated by his friends and classmates, who mocked his circumcised penis. Shortly after the analysis was terminated, he returned, complaining of some depression and a sense of disappointment that the analysis had not given him what he had expected. Further analysis disclosed an interesting fantasy. He imagined that, throughout the analysis, I had put all the money that he had paid me into a strongbox in my office. He expected that, at the end of the analysis, I would take the money out of its hiding place and give it back to him. Behind this was an unconscious fantasy that the analyst would restore his foreskin.

Even the most mundane expressions of what may happen after the analysis deserve the closest attention during the termination phase. Patients frequently conjecture on the nature of the final leave-taking and raise the question of whether they can establish a friendly or personal relationship with the analyst: Perhaps they will run into him on the street or at some social gathering; would the analyst accept an invitation to dinner?, and so on. A full chapter on analytic technique could be written about patients' fantasies of "after the analysis." Many hidden transference wishes surface in this seemingly innocent context because, after the analysis, the taboos that pertain to the professional relationship presumably no longer hold. These wishes resemble the ideas of certain religious believers who hope to attain in the afterlife what was not possible for them during their terrestrial existence. Before one facilely accepts a patient's unwillingness to separate, or his clinging to the analyst because he, the analyst, is a "new object," as the reason the patient is not ready to leave treatment, it is always advisable to examine carefully the patient's notions of what life will be like after the analysis and what lies behind these notions.

Finally, of course, there are those realistic disappointments and unjust blows of fate that the analysis is supposed to correct—persons with physical defects who want to be reborn whole, dead parents to be restored, absent parents to be avenged—the whole range of the "exceptions" as described by Freud (1916). In other words, before resorting to such concepts as the stickiness of the libido or congenital weakness of the ego, we should pay more attention to the experiential factors in the individual's life that influence the vicissitudes of instinctual development and the growth of the ego as they affect the nature of the neurotic process and the character of the transference.

The limits of what treatment can achieve are inherent not only in psychoanalysis, but in the nature of the human condition as well. Psychoanalysis cannot create a "perfect" human being, nor can it render one immune to possible neurotic illness; it cannot even assure a successfully analysed person that his neurosis will never recur. Conflict is an inevitable, unavoidable dimension of existence. As Freud said, fate may be kind to an individual and spare him ordeals too severe to master. There are, in fact, limits to the capacity for adaptation. The ego capacity of the human evolved in the context of an "average expectable environment" (Hartmann 1950) and operates only in consonance with such a setting.

The psychoanalytic situation, which is the basic research and therapeutic instrument of psychoanalysis, was devised specifically for eliciting a continuing, dynamic record of intrapsychic conflict (Freud 1925). One's interpretations concerning the influence of unconscious elements of the mind are inferences sustained by the nature and the pattern of the patient's associations as conceptualized in terms of the interplay of conflicting forces. By the very nature of its methodology, psychoanalysis can only deal with active conflicts evidenced by the derivative manifestations that appear in consciousness. A latent conflict is a hypothetical possibility which we extrapolate from our knowledge of the vicissitudes of development. Among other factors, external events of sufficiently severe intensity or of a special nature may have the capacity to disrupt a previously effective compromise formation, one that had proved satisfactory in mastering an earlier conflict. In this way, beneficial results of a successful analysis may be undone, or a new form of neurotic illness may supervene, based on the evocation of a conflict that had been in the past spontaneously mastered in the course of normal development. (It is to such problems that Hartmann [1955] directed his concepts of instinctual neutralization and deneutralization and of ego strength, as measured by the resistance to the reinstinctualization of ego functions.)

Behind the notion of a prophylactic immunization against future neurotic illness is the illusory, magical quest for eternal happiness and perfection, a fragment of childhood narcissism that we never completely surrender. Some schools of psychoanalytic thought indeed seem to suggest that such a goal may be attainable. This would appear to be the case for those who play down the role of conflict in pathogenesis in favor of the vicissitudes of development and object relations. If only the mother had done things properly and the object relations had been truly empathic, how differently things would have turned out! Such considerations quite logically influence the way the analyst treats the patient during psychoanalysis. Friedman (1978) has characterized the techniques of these analysts as a form of replacement therapy, that is, an attempt to recreate and improve the mother-child relationship of the first years of life. Treatment is effected as a recapitulation of development under more favourable conditions, with the analyst serving appropriately as a mother surrogate. In this new developmental experience, with the bad mother replaced by the good analyst, the pathological structures deriving from faulty development can be undone. Supposedly this leads to a reorganization of the psychic apparatus in a new process of development under the aegis of an appropriate, empathic, affective relationship with the therapist. According to Friedman, implicit in this approach is the notion that growth is a nonstructured phenomenon that happens automatically, if not interfered with by the noxious intrusions of the less-than-adequate unempathic mother. One outcome of such thinking may be therapeutic goals that are quite illusory in nature, for example, achieving superego functioning that is completely rational and dominated totally by secondary-process thinking or by the equally illusory belief that a mature, truly loving object relationship is totally unambivalent.

As Freud pointed out, there are limits to the prophylactic contribution to mental hygiene that psychoanalysis can make. Life makes it impossible to raise any child in a perfect manner and, even under the best of circumstances, no guarantee can be issued at one time against future psychoneurotic difficulties. Until now we have been emphasizing how external events undo the psychological equilibrium achieved through appropriate compromise formations. In the normal range of experience the contribution of the individual, particularly the role played by his fantasy life, is of equal importance to external factors in the process of pathogenesis. This is reflected in the psychoanalytic concept of trauma. Except for extreme cases of abuse far beyond the average expectable environment, trauma does not reside in the external event alone. For instance, all children who lose a parent in the first or second year of life do not respond in the same way. While such an event, like other events, represents an adaptational challenge, it is not in and of itself pathogenic. Whether an experience proves traumatic or not depends upon the individual's ability to effect a satisfactory adaptation, one that integrates into a successful compromise the elements of the conflict that the experience generates.

I believe that those analysts who center their view of human nature on the inexorable and ubiquitous nature of conflict tend to have a more realistic view than others of what can be expected from analysis. They are willing to settle for less. In "Analysis Terminable and Interminable," this is the conclusion that Freud seems finally to have reached. There he said, "Our aim will not be to rub off every peculiarity of human character for the sake of a schematic 'normality', nor yet to demand that the person who has been 'thoroughly analysed' shall feel no passions and develop no internal conflicts. The business of the analysis is to secure the best possible psychological conditions for the functions of the ego; with that it has discharged its task" (p. 250). In other words, the goal of analysis is to effect the most workable compromise among the various forces in conflict in the human mind.

In certain respects present-day views on technique diverge sharply from those that Freud held in this 1937 paper. This is particularly true in regard to the part played by the attitude of the analysand towards the analyst, that is, by whether the transference feeling towards the analyst is positive or negative. Freud says here that when the patient is confronted with the unpleasurable feelings that arise as a result of the fresh activation of his conflicts, negative transference supervenes and tends to annul the cooperation from the patient which is necessary to maintain the psychoanalytic situation. The patient refuses to listen and interpretations have no effect upon him. Freud revives here one of his earlier concepts concerning the relationship between positive and negative transference and therapeutic technique. In his technical papers, he had urged that interpretations be given only during the phase of positive transference, because then the patient would be prone to accept them, whereas, during phases of negative transference, the patient would reject interpretations offered.

This has not been borne out by experience. To begin with, as Freud himself had said on other occasions, whether the patient accepts or rejects the interpretation given by the analyst is of little consequence. What is important is the dynamic effect of the interpretation. The patient may reject some insight offered by the analyst but then come up with confirmatory material. Shall we say, in such an instance, that the initial rejection is negative transference and the subsequent production of confirmatory material constitutes positive transference? If we view transferences as vehicles of specific unconscious fantasy wishes, if they represent derivative compromises of persistent unconscious fantasy, then the whole concept of positive or negative transference is irrelevant. In fact, it seems that the terms *positive transference* and *negative transference* are outmoded and should be dropped. Material that emerges during a period when the patient feels unfriendly or hostile to the analyst may, nonetheless, serve as the basis for deepening one's insight into the patient's conflicts and for advancing the therapeutic work. So-called positive transferences may be quite beguiling and serve the purposes of resistance even more effectively than certain so-called negative transferences. Labeling the patient's productions in terms of the conscious, affective tone that permeates them skews the analysis of their meaning in favour of surface phenomena which, on examination, may turn out to serve primarily the purposes of defense. In his study "On the vicissitudes of insight in psychoanalysis," Kris (1956) has demonstrated the great range of variation of meaning that may pertain to the patient's behavior vis-à-vis the analyst.

In closing, I would like to comment on an aspect of rereading Freud's paper that I am sure I share with many colleagues. No matter how often one returns to these sources one always comes upon something new and striking, as well as something that has influenced our analytic thinking even when we were not aware of it. Freud notes that, in order to sustain the analytic situation, it is necessary for the analyst to ally himself with the ego of the person under treatment and thus subdue portions of his id which are uncontrolled. This is, of course, not possible in the case of psychotics, who do not have normal egos. Freud then goes on to say, "The ego, if we are to be able to make such a pact with it, must be a normal one. But a normal ego of this sort is, like normality in general, an ideal fiction. The abnormal ego, which is unserviceable for our purposes, is unfortunately no fiction. *Every normal person, in fact, is only normal on the average. His ego approximates to that of the psychotic in some part or other and to a greater or lesser extent;* and the degree of its remoteness from one end of the series and of its proximity to the other will furnish us with a provisional measure of what we have so indefinitely termed an 'alteration of the ego'" (p. 235, emphasis added).

In a previous essay, Brenner and I (1969) proposed that, instead of having two separate theories in psychoanalysis, one for the neuroses and another for the psychoses, we might use the structural theory to encompass the psychopathology of the psychoses. Symptoms of the psychoses could be understood in terms of conflict, defense, and compromise formation. We suggested that there is a complementary series, a range of disturbance reflecting the ego's inability to effect adequate resolution of conflicts, from the severe pathology observed in the case of the psychoses to the relatively mild disturbances observed in neurotics and the so-called normal. The problem in the psychopathology—not the aetiology—of the psychosis resides in the failure of the weak ego vis-à-vis the overpowering force of the drives. The aetiological considerations—namely, how the ego came to be so weak and the drives so powerful—remain elusive. Our ideas extend the views Freud expressed in the section of "Analysis Terminable and Interminable" quoted in the previous paragraph.

Freud raises many issues in this paper concerning the role of the analyst, his personality, and his technique, as they relate to the outcome of therapeutic work. Issues such as countertransference, empathy, psychoanalytic education, and the analyst as a model for identification must be reserved for later consideration. The wealth of ideas contained in this paper is inexhaustible and their pursuit interminable.

REFERENCES

Arlow, J.A. 1952. Discussion of Dr. Fromm-Reichmann's paper, Some aspects of psychoanalytic psychotherapy with schizophrenics. In *Psychotherapy with schizophrenics*. Edited by E. B. Brody and F. C. Redlich, 112–20. New York: International Universities Press.

———. 1969. Unconscious fantasy and disturbances of conscious experience. *Psychoanal. Q.* 38:1–27.

———. 1978. Pyromania and the primal scene: A psychoanalytic comment on the work of Yukio Mishima. *Psychoanal. Q.* 47:24–51.

Arlow, J.A., and Brenner, C., 1969. The psychopathology of the psychoses: A proposed revision. *Int. J. Psycho-Anal.* 50:5–14.

Blum, H. P. 1979. On the concept and consequences of the primal scene. *Psychoanal. Q.* 48:27–47.

Brenner, C. 1976. *Psychoanalytic techniques and psychic conflict*. New York: International Universities Press.

————. 1981. Defense and defense mechanisms. *Psychoanal. Q.* 50:557–69.

Esman, A. H. 1973. The primal scene: A review and a reconsideration. *Psychoanalytic Study of the Child* 28:49–81. New Haven and London: Yale University Press.

Freud, S. 1916. Some character-types met with in psycho-analytic work. *S.E.* 14:311–31.

————. 1923. *The ego and the id. S.E.* 19:1–59.

————. 1925. *An autobiographical study. S.E.* 20:3–70.

————. 1937. Constructions in analysis. *S.E.* 23:255–69.

————. 1940. *An outline of psycho-analysis. S.E.* 23:141–207.

Friedman, L. 1978. Trends in the psychoanalytic theory of treatment. *Psychoanal. Q.* 47:524–67.

Hartmann, H. 1939. *Ego psychology and the problem of adaptation.* New York: International Universities Press, 1958.

————. 1950. Comments on the psychoanalytic theory of the ego. In *Essays on Ego Psychology*, 113–41. New York: International Universities Press, 1964.

————. 1953. Contribution to the metapsychology of schizophrenia. *Psychoanalytic Study of the Child* 8:177–98. New York: International Universities Press.

————. 1955. Notes on the theory of sublimation. *Psychoanalytic Study of the Child* 10:9–29. New York: International Universities Press.

Kris, E. 1956. On some vicissitudes of insight in psycho-analysis. *Int. J. Psycho-Anal.* 37:445–55.

Nunberg, H. 1926. The will to recovery. In *Practice and theory of psychoanalysis: a collection of essays*, 75–88. New York: Nervous and Mental Disease Publishing Company, 1948.

Orens, M. 1955. Setting a termination date—an impetus to analysis. *J. Amer. Psychoanal. Assn.* 3:651–65.

Reich, A. 1953. Narcissistic object choice in women. *J. Amer. Psychoanal. Assn.* 1:22–44.

Schmideberg, M. 1938. After the analysis . . . *Psychoanal. Q.* 7:122–42.

Waelder, R. 1962. Psychoanalysis, scientific method and philosophy: A review. *J. Amer. Psychoanal. Assn.* 10:617–37.

Wangh, M. 1959. Structural determinants of phobia: A clinical study. *J. Amer. Psychoanal. Assn.* 7:675–95.

Analysis Finite
and Infinite

HARALD LEUPOLD-LÖWENTHAL

"Du kennest mich und dich und Tod und Leben nicht."
["Thou knowest not me or thee or death or life."]
HÖLDERLIN, *Der Tod des Empedokles*

In his notes on Freud's *Moses*, Ernest Jones (1940) wrote that someone had
once said that, like Beethoven's symphonies, Freud's writings tended to
alternate in their attitude toward the audience. In works like *Beyond the
Pleasure Principle*, Freud seemed to be writing mainly for himself and, as it
were, thinking aloud: "The audience must be content to extract what they
can from the impressive process going on and be grateful for the remarkable
privilege so vouchsafed them." The benefit to readers was then proportional
to the effort made; Freud forced them to join in the struggle. In other works,
however, he proved to be a brilliant teacher who anticipated objections and
difficulties and helped the readers.

Many of Freud's works are of the same type as *Beyond the Pleasure
Principle*. The reactions to them not only of contemporary psychoanalysts
but also of later generations have varied widely, ranging from downright
rejection to complete reinterpretation. Examples of the latter occur in sym-
posia and articles whose titles include words such as "ten," or "twenty" (or
even more) years on, or "later" — like the sequels to *The Three Musketeers*.

"Die endliche und die unendliche Analyse" was published in 1937 in
issue 2 of the *Internationale Zeitschrift für Psychoanalyse*. An English trans-

lation by Joan Riviere appeared in the same year in issue 4 of the *International Journal of Psycho-Analysis* under the title "Analysis Terminable and Interminable." In discussing the terminal phase of individual analyses, Freud here deals quite skeptically with the increasing length of analysis, its results, and its therapeutic efficacy. In his commentary in the Standard Edition, James Strachey states that this paper and its successor, "Constructions in Analysis" (1937a), were the last strictly psychoanalytic writings by Freud to be brought out in his lifetime. Nearly twenty years had passed since he had published a purely technical work, though questions of technique had, of course, been dealt with in his other writings. Even Strachey cannot escape forming an impression of Freud's pessimism, particularly in regard to the therapeutic efficacy of psychoanalysis. However, he emphasizes that, especially in the last years of his life, Freud turned his attention more to the nontherapeutic aspects of psychoanalysis: "Thus there is nothing unexpected in the cool attitude shown in this paper towards the therapeutic ambitions of psychoanalysis or in the enumeration of the difficulties confronting it" (p. 212). But he finds some features of Freud's examination of the underlying nature and causes of those difficulties surprising.

Helene Deutsch described something similar in *Confrontations with Myself*: "In his later years, Freud leaned towards the philosophical, speculative aspects of psychoanalysis[1] and thereby encouraged others toward speculation." However, this was by no means welcomed by Deutsch: "In retrospect he was moved to remark, 'For a short while I allowed myself to leave the sheltered bay of direct experience for speculation. I regret it greatly, for the consequences of so doing do not seem of the best.'"

During his address on the occasion of the opening of the new premises of the Vienna Psychoanalytical Society at Berggasse 7 on 5 May 1936, on the eve of Freud's eightieth birthday, Ernest Jones (1936a) made it clear that he was not expecting much innovation in technique: "In the field of Technique I shall be surprised if any revolutionary change is vouchsafed to us in the near future by any great discovery. At least I do not see the signs of any such on the horizon. What I look to is rather a steady progress in thoroughness, a greater polish and accuracy leading to far more sureness than we now possess."

We have no (published) documentary evidence of the importance that

---

1. See, for example, Sigmund Freud, *Civilization and Its Discontents*, trans. James Strachey (New York: W. W. Norton, 1962).

Freud himself attached to "Analysis Terminable and Interminable." After all, at the time of the writing of this paper, as in the previous year, he was occupied primarily with the essays on Moses. Thus he wrote in a letter to Oskar Pfister on 27 March 1937: "Actually I do not deserve your reproach for not writing anything. I have finished a sizeable piece about some significant matters, but because of external considerations, or rather dangers, it cannot be published. It is again about religion, so again it will not be pleasing to you. So only a few short papers have been usable for the Almanac and *Imago*" (p. 144).

Freud had written to Max Eitingon in similar terms on 5 February 1937: "Having recovered from the most recent damage and able once more to smoke to a certain extent, I have even started writing again. Just minor things: A fragment that could be detached from the work on Moses (known to you and Arnold Zweig) has been completed. The more important things connected with it must of course remain unsaid. A brief technical essay which is slowly taking shape has the function of helping me fill the many free hours with which my dwindling analytical practice has presented me." Ernest Jones (1962) believes that this essay must have been "Analysis Terminable and Interminable," while Ernst Freud (1961) suggests it was "Constructions in Analysis." Freud's mention of the Almanac and *Imago* suggests that Jones was right, as the *Almanach der Psychoanalyse 1938* includes a brief extract from "Analysis Terminable and Interminable."

The year 1936 was marked by celebrations of Freud's eightieth birthday, the need for further operations (and histological evaluation that again revealed the presence of cancerous tissue), and his golden wedding. All this, together with the increasing threat to his life and work presented by political events, aroused in Freud feelings reflected in the following passage from a letter to Arnold Zweig: "The climate of the times, and also the happenings within the International Psycho-Analytical Society, do not make us very cheerful. Austria seems bent on becoming National Socialist. Fate seems to be conspiring with that gang. With ever less regret do I wait for the curtain to fall for me." This letter, dated 22 June 1936, was followed on 2 April 1937 by one in which Freud described other anxieties that had pursued him throughout his life: "My hereditary claim on life runs out, as you know, in November. I would like to be able to guarantee it up till then, but I really do not want to delay any longer than that, for everything around us grows ever darker and more ominous and the awareness of one's own helplessness ever more pressing."

Ernest Jones writes in his biography of Freud: "Freud managed to get some writing done in 1937 in spite of his distressing condition." He refers to "Analysis Terminable and Interminable" as "for the practising psycho-analyst possibly the most valuable contribution Freud ever wrote." Nonethe-less, the publication of this paper in June 1937 was not followed by the detailed discussion that usually greeted Freud's new work, for instance, at the meetings of the Vienna Psychoanalytical Society. This omission was a response to political events and, in my view, also to the style of Freud's presentation. "Analysis Terminable and Interminable" surely belongs to the group of works, mentioned at the beginning of this essay, that, by their construction alone, cause difficulty to readers, force them to work hard, and do not present them solely with an established body of ideas. At the same time, this particular paper must be considered against the specific back-ground of contemporary political and scientific history and Freud's personal biographical circumstances and must not be misunderstood as a mere "tech-nical" discussion. The year 1974 saw the publication of an English transla-tion of a manuscript by Otto Fenichel ("A Review of Freud's 'Analysis Ter-minable and Interminable'"), which had been circulated privately—not "shortly after the original publication of Freud's paper in German" (Fenichel's editorial note), but, as the text makes clear, only in 1938. The manuscript is probably the only more or less contemporary and immediate recorded reac-tion to Freud's paper. Fenichel also discussed the paper in a series of articles entitled "Problems of Psychoanalytic Technique" published in the *Psycho-analytic Quarterly* in 1939 and in book form later (Fenichel 1941).

Freud's paper is divided into eight sections. He himself describes its logi-cal structure at the beginning of section V:

> We started from the question of how we can shorten the inconveniently long duration of analytic treatment, and, still with this question of time in mind, we went on to consider whether it is possible to achieve a permanent cure or even to prevent future illness by prophylactic treat-ment. In doing so, we found that the factors which were decisive for the success of our therapeutic efforts were the influence of traumatic aetiology, the relative strength of the instincts which have to be con-trolled, and something which we have called an alteration of the ego. Only the second of these factors has been discussed by us in any detail, and in connection with it we have had occasion to recognize the para-

mount importance of the quantitative factor and to stress the claim of the metapsychological line of approach to be taken into account in any attempt at explanation. (P. 234)

In section II, however, Freud makes a statement that seems to me to be of great importance for the assessment of his paper over and above its manifest scientific content. He speaks of alterations of the ego which call for adequate elucidation and which "are only now [in 1937] becoming the subject of analytic study" (p. 221). He continues, "In this field the interest of analysts seems to me to be quite wrongly directed. Instead of an enquiry into how a cure by analysis comes about (a matter which I think has been sufficiently elucidated) the question should be asked of what are the obstacles that stand in the way of such a cure."

Freud in 1922 had presented a paper entitled "Some Remarks on the Unconscious" at the seventh IPA Congress, in Berlin. "The speaker," an abstract reads, "discussed the two facts which show that in the ego too there is an unconscious, which behaves dynamically like the repressed unconscious: the two facts of a resistance proceeding from the ego during analysis and of an unconscious sense of guilt. He announced that in a book which was shortly to appear—*The Ego and the Id*—he had made an attempt to estimate the influence which these new discoveries must have upon our view of the unconscious."

Since publication of *The Ego and the Id* (1923), considerations of structural theory and ego theory had become increasingly important for an understanding of the psychoanalytic and therapeutic process. After publication of Anna Freud's *The Ego and the Mechanisms of Defence* (1936) and Heinz Hartmann's Vienna lectures on ego theory (1939), ego psychology increasingly had become a central aspect of the theory of psychoanalytic technique.

Franz Alexander had given a paper entitled "A Metapsychological Description of the Process of Cure" at the IPA Congress in Salzburg in 1924 (Alexander 1925), and Wilhelm Reich's detailed works on the technique of interpretation and analysis of resistances had appeared in 1927. At the twelfth Congress, in Wiesbaden, in a paper entitled "The Fate of the Ego in the Therapeutic Process" (published in 1934 as "The Fate of the Ego in Analytic Therapy") Richard Sterba had put forward the concept of therapeutic splitting of the ego, an idea that enjoyed little acceptance at the time. A number of younger analysts spoke about analytical technique from the new viewpoint of ego psychology at the thirteenth Congress, in Lucerne: Michael

Balint (1936), Melitta Schmideberg (1938), Grete Bibring (1936), and Otto Fenichel (1934). James Strachey published his most important work, "The Nature of the Therapeutic Action of Psycho-Analysis," in the *International Journal* in 1934; this appeared in German in the *Internationale Zeitschrift* in 1935 under the title "Die Grundlagen der Therapeutischen Wirkung der Psycho-analyse." Here again, structural theory was utilized in constructing a theory of interpretation (Strachey's "mutative interpretation") and in considering the process of analytical therapy.

A symposium entitled "The Theory of Therapeutic Results," chaired by Ernest Jones, was held at the fourteenth IPA Congress, in Marienbad, on 4 August 1936. The papers were as follows: Edmund Bergler, "The Theory of Therapeutic Results in Psychoanalysis" (1937); Edward Bibring, "A General Theory of Therapy" (1937); Otto Fenichel, "The Efficacy of Psychoanalytic Therapy" (1937); Edward Glover, "The Foundations of Therapeutic Results" (1937); Hermann Nunberg, "Contributions to the Theory of Therapy" (1937); and James Strachey, "The Theory of Therapeutic Results in Psychoanalysis" (1937). Those taking part in the discussion were Helene Deutsch, Fritz Perls (!), and Hanns Sachs. Sachs, as well as Rudolph Loewenstein, had also submitted written discussion notes during the year, and these, together with the papers presented at the symposium, were published in issue 1/1937 of the *Internationale Zeitschrift* (Sachs 1937; Loewenstein 1937). This issue also included René Laforgue's planned contribution to the symposium, "The Therapeutic Factor in Analytical Treatment" (1937), which was not presented, as Laforgue was unable to attend.

Hanns Sachs said in his discussion paper that the point of departure for therapeutic technique should be experience and not a systematic foundation; "otherwise there is a danger of a gulf forming between the reality of technique, which is in many respects still incomplete and in need of improvement, on the one hand, and a theory which, although refined to the utmost degree, remains infertile, on the other." Concurring with Sachs, Loewenstein emphasized that "we must subject ourselves to a long-term task—the task of patient observation dedicated with meticulous exactitude to the details."

In the remarks quoted earlier, Freud surely was opposing any theoretically based optimism, optimism not borne out by his clinical work. His attitude thus ran counter to the trend of the Marienbad symposium. His paper is in fact an indirect criticism of the matters on which analysts' interests were centered in 1936–37. In his unpublished 1938 manuscript, Fenichel gave expression to the feeling that "Analysis Terminable and Interminable" lacked the well-rounded, compelling execution customary in his earlier clinical works. He also saw Freud's choice of this topic in the light of the Marienbad symposium.

In Section V of the paper, Freud turns to the factor of alteration of the ego. At the outset he finds that there is much to ask and much to answer here and comments that "what we have to say about it will prove to be very inadequate" (p. 234). Referring to what would now be called the "therapeutic alliance" between the analyst and the patient, Freud says of the patient: "The ego, if we are to be able to make such a pact with it, must be a normal one. But a normal ego of this sort is, like normality in general, an ideal fiction. The abnormal ego, which is unserviceable for our purposes, is unfortunately no fiction" (p. 235).

Freud goes on to describe the role of the mechanisms of defense in ego development and also their significance for alterations of the ego. In this connection, he refers to Anna Freud's book *The Ego and the Mechanisms of Defence* (1936), which had just been published. Great importance attaches to the statement that the presence of the mechanisms of defense dictates part of our analytic task, namely, uncovering and countering resistances. The other part, "first tackled by analysis in its early days," Freud notes, is "the uncovering of what is hidden in the id." He elaborates, "During the treatment our therapeutic work is constantly swinging backwards and forwards like a pendulum between a piece of id-analysis and a piece of ego-analysis. In the one case we want to make something from the id conscious, in the other we want to correct something in the ego" (p. 238).

In Section VI, Freud first points out that the properties of the ego that we encounter in the form of resistances can equally well be determined by heredity as acquired in defensive struggles. This, he argues, deprives the topographical distinction between ego and id of "much of its value for our investigation." Unconscious guilt feelings, masochism, a negative therapeutic reaction, an unconscious need for punishment—all of these are sources of resistance and impediments to therapeutic success. "Here we are dealing with the ultimate things which psychological research can learn about: the behaviour of the two primal instincts, their distribution, mingling and defusion—things which we cannot think of as being confined to a single province of the mental apparatus, the id, the ego or the super-ego" (p. 242).

Freud considers that it would be "the most rewarding achievement of psychological research" (p. 243) to elucidate how parts of the two classes of instincts—Eros and the death-instinct—combine to fulfill the various vital functions, under what conditions such combinations grow looser, and the like. At this point, Freud again introduces the dualistic theory of instincts, and it is clear that he has a particular intention in so doing: "I am well aware that the dualistic theory according to which an instinct of death or of destruction or aggression claims equal rights as a partner with Eros as manifested in the libido, has found little sympathy and has not really been accepted even among psycho-analysts." He continues: "This made me all the more pleased when not long ago I came upon this theory of mine in the writings of one of the great thinkers of ancient Greece" (pp. 244–45). He is "very ready to give up the prestige of originality," as "our" theory was discussed by analysts only reluctantly—most recently at a joint meeting of the Vienna Psychoanalytical Society, the Hungarian Psychoanalytical Society, the Italian Psychoanalytical Society (which did not yet belong to the IPA), and the Czechoslovak Society of Prague, a study group (*Arbeitsgemeinschaft*) of the Vienna Society, the "four-country meeting" (*Vierländertagung*) held in Vienna at Whitsun 1935. It was an exceptionally successful meeting.

The first of a series of "scientific symposiums" was held in Vienna at the premises of the Wirtschaftliche Organisation der Ärzte (Economic Organization of Physicians) on 9 June 1935 and was chaired by István Hollós. The main paper, presented by Edoardo Weiss, was entitled "The Death Instinct and Masochism." The following notes appear in the "Leitlinien" (Outline) published in the Korrespondenzblatt (Bulletin) of the IPA: "Inadequacy of the theoretical foundation of the death instinct; phenomena which argue in favour of its existence," or "the supposed death instinct and the field of validity of the pleasure-unpleasure principle," or again, "Masochism presupposes the existence of destructive instinctual energy (destrudo), which, must not, however, necessarily be regarded as the expression of a "death instinct," probable as this may be." Contributors to the discussion were Hartmann, Eidelberg, Federn, M. Balint, Waelder, and Weiss. The subject of the second symposium was "Psychic Trauma and the Handling of the Transference." Papers were presented by Sterba and A. Balint (1935). On 10 June 1935, in the third symposium, chaired by Francis Deri, Robert Waelder presented a paper entitled "Problems of Ego Psychology" (1935). The Leitlinien noted: "The rejection of psychoanalysis in the outside world was and is based on the rejection of id psychology; the same applies to the first secession movements." It remarked on "the inadequacy of any psychoanalytic explanation without ego psychology," and "the problem of ego strength, its conditions and ways of promoting it pedagogically and thera-peutically." The discussants were Bibring, Kris, Hartmann, Hermann, A. Reich, Federn, M. Balint, Weiss, Hollós, Stengel, A. Balint, and Waelder.

The choice of subject matter and the discussion at the four-country meet-ing show to what extent Freud, in "Analysis Terminable and Interminable," was in fact entering into the contemporary scientific controversy of 1936–37, very clearly pointing the way ahead with the signposts that were important to him. He had done something similar in *The Ego and the Id* (1923) in reemphasizing in chapter 4 ("The Two Classes of Instincts") the importance of the theory of instincts and, in particular, of the "fundamental dualistic point of view": "At the same time the ego is subject to the influence of the instincts, too, like the id, of which it is, as we know, only a specially modified part." His aim in the 1937 paper was the same.

The "great thinker of ancient Greece" to whom Freud referred was Empedocles of Acragas. Freud had read of him in volume 119, *Die Vorsokratiker, die Fragmente und Quellenberichte* (The pre-Socratics: frag-ments and source material), of Kröner's pocket editions, intended to make specialized sources available to a wider public. Wilhelm Capelle translated the material and wrote an introduction (Capelle 1935), using as his princi-pal foundation the work of Hermann Diels.

Freud's summary of the ideas of Empedocles is taken from Capelle's introduction. He justifies his detailed description of these ideas as follows: "But the theory of Empedocles which especially deserves our interest is one which approximates so closely to the psycho-analytic theory of the instincts that we should be tempted to maintain that the two are identical, if it were not for the difference that the Greek philosopher's theory is a cosmic phan-tasy while ours is content to claim biological validity" (p. 245). Freud was also impressed by Empedocles as a man, describing him as "one of the grandest and most remarkable figures" of the pre-Socratic period. He men-tions that Capelle compared Empedocles to Dr. Faust, a man "to whom many a secret was revealed," an inquirer with an intense thirst to explore the ultimate causes of nature and at the same time an out-and-out super-naturalist—as Faust says, one "dedicated to magic."

Empedocles was a subject of legendary anecdotes, and the story of his life is adorned with mythical embellishments. For instance, his death far from home in the Peloponnese remains shrouded in obscurity, and it was thought that he had been carried off to the Elysian Fields. His jealous opponents, however, put it about that he had ended his life by leaping into the volcano Etna, by this mysterious disappearance to make people believe that he had been transported to the realm of the gods. The profound symbolic significance of this story had a powerful impact on Hölderlin, who wrote three versions of a tragedy entitled *Der Tod des Empedokles* (The death of Empedocles).

In the *Outline* (1940), Freud's last, unfinished work, he mentions Empedocles again in a footnote to the chapter "The Theory of the Instincts": "This picture of the basic forces or instincts, which still arouses much opposition among analysts, was already familiar to the philosopher Empedocles of Acragas." Empedocles was certainly "The Great Man" as described by Freud in *Moses and Monotheism*. Freud concerned himself for a long time with Moses, an identificatory figure of great importance to him, and he clearly saw Empedocles as a reincarnation of Moses. Perhaps this is why, in a letter to Martin Freud written on 16 August 1937, he recalled a visit he had made to Capri in 1902, with his brother Alexander: "Vesuvius was also active, producing a smoke cloud by day and a fire cloud by night, just like the God of Exodus in the Bible. For Jehovah (Jahve) was a volcanic god, as you will learn from the second essay on Moses, which is now finished, awaiting your return" (see also the footnote in *S.E.* 23:45–46).

The particular importance that Freud attached to Section VI of "Analysis Terminable and Interminable" is clearly revealed by the fact that the *Almanach der Psychoanalyse 1938* reproduced no other than Freud's discussion of Empedocles as "a brief extract" under the title "Analysis Terminable and Interminable."

Freud's intention was clearly to forestall any dogmatism in the matter of termination of analysis and to prevent (as it turned out, relatively successfully) new theoretical insights from setting prematurely into hard and fast technical requirements and rules. He also attempted to preserve the central position of the theory of instincts in the work of psychoanalysis and once again put forth the theory of the death instinct for discussion on a large scale. However, in "Analysis Terminable and Interminable" he now distanced himself from his earlier metaphor of psychoanalysis as a game of chess (Freud 1913) in which the opening and the end game were fixed, move by move, and only the unregulated middle game presented technical difficulties.

Although Freud had drawn attention as early as 1926 to the importance of phase-specific anxieties (loss of object, separation anxiety, loss of love, and castration) and their role in subsequent pathology, few of his views on developmental psychology can still be found in "Analysis Terminable and Interminable." This was perhaps because (as Helen Tartakoff also assumes) he still adhered to the classical model of symptom analysis, although he had described the complexity of the personality as a whole many years before. But the significance of the paper lies not so much in its pragmatism and the technical suggestions it contains, as in its emphasis on the importance of restraint and caution in the translation of (new) theoretical positions into technical practice.

In section VII of his paper, Freud again refers to the importance of time as an element in psychoanalysis. His starting point is Sándor Ferenczi's "instructive" paper on the problem of the termination of analyses, presented at the tenth IPA Congress, in Innsbruck in 1927. Ferenczi had emphasized the element of time in postulating that in effect analysis required endless time—not in physical terms but in the psychological sense of a decision to "really carry on for as long as proves to be necessary, regardless of the absolute duration of time." But at the same time, as Freud stresses, Ferenczi ended with the comforting assurance that "'analysis is not an endless process, but one which can be brought to a natural end with sufficient skill and patience on the analyst's part'" (p. 247). Freud adds: "The paper as a whole, however, seems to me to be in the nature of a warning not to aim at shortening analysis but at deepening it."

Freud had explained this in a letter to Arnold Zweig dated 13 June 1935, in connection with Zweig's analysis:

> A proper analysis is a slow process. In some cases I myself have only been able to uncover the core of the problem after many years, not, it is true, of continuous analysis, and I was not able to say where I had gone wrong in my technique. It is the exact opposite of a mountebank like O. Rank who travels around maintaining that he can cure a severe obsessional neurosis in four months! But partial and superficial analyses, such as you are having, are also fruitful and beneficial. The main impression one gets is of the marvellous quality of the life of the psyche. But it is a scientific undertaking rather than an easy therapeutic operation.

Freud implies in this letter that the work of analysis is not, or not only, effective as a therapeutic intervention but, being "rather" a scientific undertaking, clearly also makes insights possible.

He does, on the other hand, make it clear in his 1937 paper that he has no intention of asserting that analysis is altogether an endless business: "Whatever one's theoretical attitude to the question may be, the termination of an analysis is, I think a practical matter" (p. 249). This is consistent with Ferenczi's view that, in an analysis that takes a normal course, the conditions for the termination are automatically satisfied and "the analysis as it were dies of exhaustion." Freud considers the practical task of psychoanalysis to have been discharged when it has secured the best possible psychological conditions for the functions of the ego. However, if only for the analyst himself, Freud has to express the hope that "the processes of remodelling the ego [will continue] spontaneously in the analysed subject and [that he will make] use of all subsequent experiences in this newly-acquired sense" (p. 249). For the analyst Freud suggests the possibility of periodic re-analysis: "This would mean, then, that not only the therapeutic analysis of patients but his own analysis would change from a terminable into an interminable task" (p. 249).

The terminable task of therapeutic analysis is here compared with the possibility of an interminable analysis for particular classes of patients, such as practicing analysts. The need for an interminable prolongation of the analytic process follows to some extent from the particular nature of the work of analysis because, first, "Among the factors which influence the prospects of analytic treatment and add to its difficulties in the same manner as the resistances, must be reckoned not only the nature of the patient's ego but the individuality of the analyst" (p. 247). A second consideration is that analysis as a profession has its dangers, which Freud compares with the effect of X-rays (p. 249).

Freud clearly did not have a very high opinion of the analytic training of his time, which had become increasingly institutionalized, and he also had little confidence in the favorable effects of the training analysis. He had remarked on this to Lou Andreas-Salomé on 6 January 1935: "My one source of satisfaction is Anna. It is remarkable how much influence and authority she has gained among the general run of analysts — many of whom, alas, have derived little from analysis as far as their personal character is concerned."

In a paper on the termination of analysis, Ernst Ticho (1971) underlines the importance of distinguishing between the goals of treatment and life goals. He in turn distinguishes between professional and personal life goals. In the case of a psychoanalyst, it seems to be particularly difficult to separate adequately the professional part of the life goals from the goals of treatment in such a way that a satisfying termination of the (training) analysis can be achieved. This is surely also the background to Ticho's point that there is plenty of clinical evidence suggesting further growth after the conclusion of analysis. He adds: "It is our assumption that growth takes place all through life, and that the removal of obstructions to growth opens the way for increased maturity."

Maria Kramer (1959) takes the subject of the "terminability" of the analytic process a step further in her paper "On the Continuation of the Analytic Process after Psychoanalysis (A Self-Observation)." Her starting point is Freud's hope for continuation of the processes of remodeling the ego in the analyzed subject. (She quotes this sentence in the original German in a footnote and substitutes an English translation of her own for that of the *Standard Edition*.) She postulates that the instrument of analysis, the "continuing analytic processes," becomes a new ego function during the course of the analytic process, although this function substantially escapes conscious control. Achievement of this self-analytic ego function depends on the release of anticathectic energy ("countercathexis").

Gertrude Ticho (1967) takes the view that, for the practicing psychoanalyst, the tension between the ego and the ego ideal might furnish the motive power for self-analysis. Awareness of the fact that working quality is impaired by unconscious conflicts promotes the obligation of self-analysis. Conversely, "The deep satisfaction and gratification provided by mastery of a conflict, and the observation of one's own growth, turn self-analysis into a never-ending process."

This attitude seems not as mistaken as it appeared to be to those many authors who regarded termination of the therapeutic analysis as an essential part of a job well done if we consider the analytic process an interaction in which the patient integrates his self-understanding, and so to speak "verifies" it, in acts of self-reflection and consequent insight (Dahmer 1973). In this process the patient acquires a certain reflective knowledge and is subsequently better able to extricate himself from the repetition compulsion.

At this point it becomes important to look at the exact formulation of Freud's title, in German "Die endliche und die unendliche Analyse." This is not rendered exactly by the English translation, nor by those that followed it into French, Spanish, Italian, and Portuguese, which have used such words as *terminable, terminée,* and *interminable.* The German words *endlich* and *unendlich* have a number of connotations that correspond only partially and inexactly with *terminable* and *interminable*.

In the German literary and philosophical tradition, the antithetical pair *endlich–unendlich* has particular significance. This is clear for example, in Goethe's often-quoted couplet from the *Sprüche in Reimen*:

> Willst du ins Unendliche schreiten,
> Geh' nur im Endlichen nach allen Seiten.
> [If thou wilt step into the infinite,
> Just explore every path in the finite.]

However, the next two lines, which are seldom quoted, are also relevant here:

> Willst du dich am Ganzen erquicken,
> So musst du das Ganze im Kleinsten erblicken
> [If thou will feast on the whole,
> Thou must seek the whole in the smallest.]

In his paper, Freud uses the relevant pair of words only in the title and at the point quoted earlier, where he says that for patient and analyst psychoanalysis might "change from a terminable [*endlich*] into an interminable [*unendlich*] task."

The words *terminable* and *interminable* are used in the *Standard Edition* and throughout the translation of Freud's paper (even where he used the words *Abschluss* [conclusion], *Ende* [end], *Beendigung* [termination], and so forth). Where Freud's original version states that both the analyst's own analysis and the therapeutic analysis of the patient would become infinite instead of finite tasks, the translation states that both "would *change* [my emphasis] from a terminable into an interminable task." The translation has thus introduced the idea of a change, which Freud did not contribute in this pragmatic sense. But this gives rise to a certain difficulty in understanding what is so important to Freud apart from and in spite of all considerations concerning the termination and terminability of analysis!

Gertrude Ticho (1967) correctly concludes: "Freud states clearly that for the psychoanalytic practitioner, analysis is an interminable task." In using the word *interminable*, she is no doubt following standard translation practice but means *unendlich* (infinite). She also quotes Willie Hoffer (1950), who suggested that a criterion of the treatment should be "identification within the ego with the function of the analyst, when the analytic process can hopefully be entrusted to the apprentice himself." Here, the *unendlich* (infinite, unending) analytic process (now not only in the setting of analytic therapy) becomes a developmental task, which fits in perfectly with Freud's cultural tradition and humanistic educational ideal.

Ernest Jones expressed similar ideas in his introduction to a British Psycho-Analytical Society symposium in London in March 1936 on "The Criteria of Success in Treatment" (1936b): "Analytical success goes beyond the pathological field altogether. It betokens an understanding . . . of the development of all the subject's main interests in life [E. Ticho's "life goals"?] . . . so that ultimately one can see his whole life as a gradual unfolding of a relatively few primary sources of interest."

Fenichel (1974) noted in his review that Freud raised the question of "analysis interminable" only in connection with the training analysis. He regards Freud's comments as insufficiently comprehensive and surprisingly skeptical. At the same time, he feels that Freud's concept of the training analysis is substantially at variance with that held by training institutes. Fenichel then discusses a pragmatic attitude to the training analysis in psychoanalytic training, based purely on the curative function of the future analyst. "If Freud expects much from the subsequent analysis of the analyst, why not equally much from the first training analysis?" Here he misunderstands Freud's dictum of "terminable and interminable work." The therapeutic work, in his view, is never an "interminable task," even in so-called character analyses.

In an essay published in 1982 Bruno Bettelheim quotes from the *New Introductory Lectures* (Freud 1933). There Freud declares that the intention of psychoanalysis is to strengthen the ego, "so that it can appropriate fresh portions of the id. Where id was, there ego shall be. It is a work of culture —not unlike the draining of the Zuider Zee." Further, since we know that Goethe played a dominant role in Freud's intellectual development, it is not mere speculation that Freud selected the metaphor of the reclamation of land from the sea because it would induce the reader to relate the work of psychoanalysis to *Faust*, the great poem about the reclamation of the soul.

Goethe's work depicts the hundred-year-old Faust, stricken with blindness by Care, indefatigably going on with his work—land drainage—while Mephisto and the Lemures are already digging his grave. He thinks "the clash of spades" has to do with his "projected locks and dykes" and feels that he has accomplished the object of his striving:

FAUST: Then to the moment could I say:
　　　　Linger you now, you are so fair!
　　　　Now records of my earthly day
　　　　No flight of aeons can impair—
　　　　Foreknowledge comes, and fills me with such bliss,
　　　　I take my joy, my highest moment this.

But with these words, according to his pact with Mephisto, he forfeits his life, and Mephisto believes he has achieved *his* aim:

MEPHISTO: Time wins, with Greybeard stretched out on the sand.
　　　　The clock stands still—
CHORUS:　 It stands as midnight stilled,
　　　　The finger falls.
MEPHISTO: It falls, all is fulfilled.
CHORUS:　 It is bygone.
MEPHISTO: A foolish word, bygone.
　　　　How so then gone?
　　　　Gone, to sheer Nothing, past with null made one!

Mephisto does not see the outcome of his struggle in the "finite" (*endlich*), in the achievement of a goal; he knows about the impossibility of a termination. As in the eternal struggle between Empedocles' *philia* and *neikos*, in which now one and then the other of these two principles is victorious, it is a matter of an unending [*unendlich*] process. For Empedocles this process rested on the foundation of the compelling law of Ananke. Freud took up this view again for the purposes of his dualistic theory of instincts in "Analysis Terminable and Interminable" and defended it powerfully—as Fenichel put it, in a "digression," "the length of which is in contrast to its significance for the problem under discussion." But this is only the case if a purely pragmatic and technical standpoint is adopted, and it is becoming increasingly clear that this was only a secondary consideration for Freud at this point.

Goethe's Faust is saved and Mephisto is robbed of his victory. The final scene, which, in Goethe's own words to Eckermann (6 June 1831), "contains the key to Faust's salvation," includes these lines:

　　　　For he whose strivings never cease
　　　　Is ours for his redeeming.

However, Faust's survival, the unending nature of his striving, is not to be understood as "eternal bliss" in the sense of the Christian afterlife, but is a new, heightened form of activity, a metamorphosis that takes place in unending movement, a constant struggle between powers signifying a continuous struggling to reach perfection.

Bettelheim says that our struggle between the life and death instincts in ourselves explains the manifold nature of human life and gives life its deepest meaning. Freud's words were these: "Only by the concurrent or mutually opposing action of the two primal instincts—Eros and the death-instinct—, never by one or the other alone, can we explain the rich multiplicity of the phenomena of life" (p. 243).

P. Meisel and W. Kendrick (1968) say in the epilogue to their edition of the letters of James and Alix Strachey: "Any translator knows that pedantic exactitude in the rendering of individual terms is ultimately both self-defeating and pernicious. The reason is a straightforward one: translation, if it is to succeed, must reimagine the texts it translates. Freud's works are in some sense a précis of the entire German cultural tradition; to make him English required the establishment of an equivalence rather than a correspondence."

We certainly agree with their subsequent statement that the Stracheys succeeded in this task and that "no one will see their like again." But it is important to note that in the effort "to make Freud English" in the specific case of "Analysis Terminable and Interminable," the essential aspects of the cultural background and of the contemporary scientific controversy, to which Freud merely alluded, in fact found only equivalence. "Analysis Terminable and Interminable" actually contains something more than they were able to convey; it is the testament of a dying man who wanted to show once again what he held to be so important.

At the meeting of 20 March 1930 held to discuss *Civilization and its Discontents*, Freud compared his book to the Tropaeum of Anaklisse: " 'Analysis Terminable and Interminable' possesses a similarly remarkable composition: a narrow tropaeum surmounts a rather diffuse, broad substructure" (quoted in Sterba 1982). The description is equally applicable to this paper:

> My book is the outcome of the insight that our theory of instincts was insufficient. It has been said that I am trying to force the death instinct upon analysts. However, I am only like an old farmer who plants fruit trees, or like someone who has to go out of the house and leaves a toy behind so that the children will have something to play with while he is absent. I wrote the book with purely analytic intentions, based on my former existence as an analytic writer, in brooding

contemplation, concerned to promote the concept of the feeling of guilt to its very end. The feeling of guilt is created by the renunciation of aggression. Now it's up to you to play with this idea. But I consider this the most important progress in analysis.

I wonder if we, too, ought not to play again.

REFERENCES

Alexander, F. 1925. A metapsychological description of the process of cure. *Int. J. Psycho-Anal.* 6:13–34.

Balint, A. 1935. Das psychische Trauma und die Handhabung der Übertragung. Referat auf der Vierlädertagung: Leitlinien. *Int. Ztschr. Psychoanal.* 21:458–59.

Balint, M. 1936. The final goal of psycho-analytic treatment. *Int. J. Psycho-Anal.* 17:206–16.

Bergler, E. 1937. Symposium on the theory of the therapeutic results of psychoanalysis. *Int. J. Psycho-Anal.* 18:146–60.

Bettelheim, B. 1982. *Freud and man's soul.* New York: Alfred A. Knopf.

Bibring, E. 1937. Versuch einer allgemeinen Theorie der Heilung. *Int. Ztschr. Psychoanal.* 23:18–37.

Bibring-Lehner, G. 1936. A contribution to the subject of transference-resistance. *Int. J. Psycho-Anal.* 17:181–89.

Capelle, W. 1935. *Die Vorsokratiker, die Fragmente und Quellenberichte.* Leipzig: Kröner.

Dahmer, H. 1973. *Libido und Gesellschaft.* Frankfurt: Suhrkamp.

Deutsch, H. 1973. *Confrontations with myself.* New York: W. W. Norton.

Fenichel, O. 1934. Defense against anxiety, particularly by libidinization. In *The collected papers of Otto Fenichel,* 1st ser., 303–17. New York: W. W. Norton, 1953.

———. 1937. Symposium on the theory of the therapeutic results of psychoanalysis. *Int. J. Psycho-Anal.* 18:133–38.

———. 1941. *Problems of psychoanalytic technique.* New York: Psychoanalytic Quarterly, Inc.

———. 1974. A review of Freud's 'Analysis terminable and interminable.' *Int. Rev. Psycho-Anal.* 1:109–116.

Ferenczi, S. 1927. The problem of the termination of the analysis. In *Final contributions to the problems and methods of psycho-analysis.* New York: Basic Books, 1955.

Freud, A. 1936. *The ego and the mechanisms of defence.* London: Hogarth.

Freud, E. L. 1961. *Letters of Sigmund Freud, 1873–1939.* London: Hogarth.

Freud, S. 1913. On beginning the treatment (further recommendations on the technique of psycho-analysis, I). *S.E.* 12:121–44.

———. 1922. Some remarks on the unconscious. Paper presented at the seventh IPA Congress, Berlin. Abstract in *Int. Ztschr. Psychoanal.* 7:486. Published later in the Editors' Introduction to *The ego and the id* (1923), *S.E.* 19:3–11.

———. 1923. *The ego and the id. S.E.* 19:19–27.

———. 1926. *Inhibitions, symptoms and anxiety. S.E.* 20:77–174.

———. 1930. Notes on *Civilization and its discontents* from a meeting at Berggasse 19, on 20 March 1930. In *Reminiscences of a Viennese psychoanalyst*, by R. Sterba. Detroit: Wayne State University Press, 1982.

———. 1933. *New introductory lectures on psycho-analysis. S.E.* 22:3–182.

———. 1937a. Constructions in analysis. *S.E.* 23:255–69.

———. 1937b. Moses an Egyptian. *S.E.* 23:7–16.

———. 1937c. If Moses was an Egyptian . . . *S.E.* 23:17–53.

———. 1938. Reprinting of part VI of Analysis terminable and interminable. *Almanach der Psychoanalyse, 1938*. Vienna: Psychoanal. Verlag.

———. 1940. *An outline of psycho-analysis. S.E.* 23:141–207.

Glover, E. 1937. Symposium on the theory of therapeutic results of psycho-analysis. *Int. J. Psycho-Anal.* 18:125–32.

Hartmann, H. 1939. *Ego psychology and the problem of adaptation.* New York: International Universities Press, 1958.

Hoffer, W. 1950. Three psychological criteria for the termination of treatment. *Int. J. Psycho-Anal.* 31:194–95.

Hölderlin, F. 1973. *Der Tod des Empedokles.* 2d ed. Stuttgart: Reclam.

Jones, E. 1936a. The future of psycho-analysis. Paper read at opening of the new premises of the Vienna Institute of Psycho-Analysis (Berggasse 7) on 5 May 1936. *Int. J. Psycho-Anal.* 17:269–77.

———. 1936b. The criteria of success in treatment. Introduction to a symposium of the British Psycho-Analytical Society. In *Papers on psycho-analysis.* 5th ed. London: Baillière, Tindall and Cox, 1948.

———. 1940. Review of Freud's *Moses and monotheism. Int. J. Psycho-Anal.* 21:230–40.

———. 1962. *Sigmund Freud: Life and work*, vol. 3. London: Hogarth, 1953.

Kramer, M. 1959. On the contribution of the analytic process after psycho-analysis (a self-observation). *Int. J. Psycho-Anal.* 40:17–25.

Laforgue, R. 1937. Der Heilungsfaktor der psychoanalytischen Behandlung. *Int. Ztschr. Psychoanal.* 23:50–59.

Leupold-Löwenthal, H. 1981. Die Beendigung der psychoanalytischen Behandlung. *Jahrbuch der Psychoanalyse*, Band 12:192–203.

Loewenstein, R. 1937. Bemerkungen zur Theorie des therapeutischen Vorganges der Psycholanalyse. *Int. Ztschr. Psychoanal.* 23:560–63.

Meisel, P., and Kendrick, W. 1986. *Bloomsbury/Freud: The letters of James and Alix Strachey, 1924–1925*. London: Chatto and Windus.

Meng, H., and Freud, E. L. 1963. *Psycho-analysis and faith: The letters of Sigmund Freud and Oskar Pfister*. London: Hogarth.

Nunberg, H. 1937. Beiträge zur Theorie der Therapie. *Int. Ztschr. Psychoanal.* 23:60–67.

Reich, W. 1927. Zur Technik der Deutung und der Widerstandsanalyse. Über die gesetzmäßige Entwicklung der Übertragungsneurose. *Int. Ztschr. Psychoanal.* 13:142–159.

Sachs, H. 1937. Zur theorie der psychoanalytischen Technik. *Int. Ztschr. Psychoanal.* 23:563.

Schmideberg, M. 1938. The mode of operation of psycho-analytic therapy. *Int. J. Psycho-Anal.* 19:310–20.

Sterba, R. 1934. The fate of the ego in analytic therapy. *Int. J. Psycho-Anal.* 15:117–26.

———. 1982. *Reminiscences of a Viennese psychoanalyst*. Detroit: Wayne State University Press.

Strachey, J. 1934. The nature of the therapeutic action of psychoanalysis. *Int. J. Psycho-Anal.* 15:27–159.

———. 1937. Zur Theorie der therapeutischen Resultate der Psychoanalyse. *Int. Ztschr. Psychoanal.* 23:69–74.

Ticho, E. 1972. Termination of psychoanalysis: Treatment goals, life goals. *Psychoanal. Q.* 41:315–33.

Ticho, G. 1967. On self-analysis. *Int. J. Psycho-Anal.* 48:308–18.

Vierländertagung. 1935. (Österreich, Ungarn, Italien, Tschechoslowakei.) [A conference of four countries (1935): Austria, Hungary, Italy, Czechoslovakia.] Report in Korrespondenzblatt der Internationalen Psychoanalytischen Vereinigung. *Int. Ztschr. Psychoanal.* 21:457–60.

Waelder, R. 1935. Problematik der Ich-Psychologie. Leitlinien. *Int. Ztschr. Psychoanal.* 21:459–60.

Weiss, E. 1935. Todestrieb und Masochismus. Leitlinien. *Int. Ztschr. Psychoanal.* 21:458.

On Teaching
"Analysis Terminable
and Interminable"

DAVID ZIMMERMANN

&

A. L. BENTO MOSTARDEIRO

Freud's "Analysis Terminable and Interminable" has been regarded as a sort of scientific "last will and testament." In the final years of his life, when he wrote this work revising and evaluating psychoanalysis, what must his prevalent feelings have been? Although his intelligence remained lucid and his creative capacity intact until practically his last moment, from time to time he gave signs that he knew his end was near. In addition, with the coming of Nazism, the keen enemy both of Jews and of psychoanalysis—which was considered a "Jewish science"—and consequent persecution in Germany and Austria, countries where psychoanalysis had prospered, Freud may have thought that the science he had created and developed might also be coming to an end. Would he have had the feeling that the world was ending? (See Jones 1957.)

FREUD'S INTERNAL AND EXTERNAL SITUATION
AT THE TIME OF WRITING THE WORK

Some well-known facts enable us to picture what might have been occurring in Freud's internal and external reality. He was eighty-one years old when

"Analysis Terminable and Interminable" was published, and he had undergone thirty-three operations on his mouth, with little reduction of the pain he had been suffering for fourteen years. Besides the progressive deterioration of his health and the diagnosis of a malignant growth, he had lost several followers and friends, as well as close family members (Grotjahn 1966). Karl Abraham had died in Berlin at the end of 1925. Freud lost in him a great friend, one who was learned and intelligent, with a sharp capacity for discernment and common sense; Abraham was someone, Freud thought, who truly "knew people." In 1930, Freud's ninety-five-year-old mother died. In a letter to Ferenczi, Freud wrote, "As to me, with the congratulations I receive for the [Goethe] Prize and the condolences addressed to me for my fatal disease and now for the death of my mother, not counting the trouble it gives me to quit smoking, I cannot do anything at all" (Robert 1964). There is no doubt that the highly significant loss of his mother, when he himself was ill, affected Freud profoundly.

In 1933, soon after the Nazis seized power in Germany, Ferenczi died. He had been Freud's best-loved companion and collaborator. Freud had called this "romantic" *enfant terrible* of psychoanalysis his "beloved son." By this point, however, Ferenczi had no more than bitter resentment for his previously beloved master, as he felt he had been poorly analyzed by the man he had venerated above everyone else (Lorand 1966). In the same year Freud was informed about the *auto-da-fé* held by the Nazis in Berlin—the public burning of his books—and this led him to state, quoting a poet, that he had "ceased understanding the world!" (Robert 1964).

The Deutsche Algemeine Ärztliche Gesellschaft für Psychotherapie came under Nazi control in June 1933 (Jones 1957). Its acting president, the renowned Professor Kretschmer, at once resigned from his position and was replaced by Carl Jung. Jung's assigned task was to draw a scientific dividing line between "Aryan psychology" and "Jewish psychology"—that is, between his own "collective unconscious" theory and Freud's psychoanalysis, against which Jung could now take easy vengeance (Robert 1964). In 1936, Dr. Goering, a cousin of the Nazi air marshal of the same name, was appointed director of the Berlin Psychological Society. In the following year the Vienna Society also came under Nazi control. Next the Verlag, which had published Freud's complete works, was sequestered, his books were destroyed, and the Vienna Psychoanalytical Society was dissolved (Robert 1964).

SUBTHEMES IN "ANALYSIS TERMINABLE AND INTERMINABLE"

"Analysis Terminable and Interminable" continues to be important, not only for the beginner, but for the practicing psychoanalyst as well, as it deals with central and basic analytic issues. These include the following: the origin of the neuroses, the duration of analysis and its termination, the constitutional strength of the drives, the possibility of patients' avoiding further psychic conflict, the alteration of ego structures and the selection of defense mechanisms, the origin of variations in ego structure, the personality of the analyst and the repudiation of the analyst's femininity. It is evident that many of the problems and questions the paper poses were clarified for the first time, while others remain obscure to this day.

The Duration of the Analysis

In the first section of the work Freud discusses the duration of the analytic process and the fact that, to that time, every attempt to shorten it has been frustrated. Otto Rank considered neurosis to be a recurrence of the birth trauma, and Freud criticized him for limiting the goals of the analysis to solving the consequences of this primal trauma. Freud compares a view such as Rank's to trying to extinguish a blazing fire simply by removing an overturned lamp from the room where the fire had started (pp. 216–17).

Here Freud seems to be ignoring his own teachings about the process of personality formation, for the personality and current condition of the patient have multiple origins and are dependent for a starting point not on one fire, but on several. However, in the rest of the work, he examines a number of factors that affect the duration of the analysis. Probably Rank's wish to find a way of shortening analysis arose in part from his notion of illness as something opposed to health—just as poverty is opposed to wealth. In part, too, the wish arose from his ignoring concerns about death connected with the notion of illness, as well as the wish to transpose to analysis the concept of focal disease and focal therapy.

Freud reports his own attempts to shorten the length of analysis and also to resolve analyses that were stagnant, analyses in which the patient had shown improvement with regard to symptoms, had solved problems, but which had then appeared to come to a standstill. In such cases the patient is comfortable in the analysis and does not intend to stop it, but at the same time he does not progress. Freud used the "trick" of setting a deadline for the completion of the analysis, intending to motivate the patient to overcome resistances and work out his problems. He cautioned, however, that the analyst had to adhere rigidly to such a deadline or risk becoming discredited.

Standstills in the analytic process are probably due to the patient's inability to endure separation anxiety; the patient prefers to allow the analysis to become stagnant rather than to face its termination. Moreover, he or she may not be able to endure the loss of the infantile rewards of keeping the analysis going and thus avoids the breakdown of the transference neurosis (Glover 1955).

In setting a date for termination of the analysis, the analyst forces the patient to face the frustration of eventually losing the infantile rewards he or she receives from his analysis. Simultaneously, setting a date forces the patient to confront separation anxiety. The analyst asks the patient to work out the fantasy of separation within a time limit imposed by the analyst (Gaburri 1985). Of course a demand of this sort works differently for a patient who has been in analysis for, say, twelve years than for one who has been analyzed for only two years. At harvest time the fruit of the twelve-year analysis should be much riper, and the setting of a deadline should result in much easier picking, than in the other case.

The analytic process, like the life process, has to go through its natural stages, and the analyst knows that skipping stages in the individual's developmental process leads to damage in personality formation. Such damage, perhaps negligible at the beginning, tends to reappear later, and the analysis, itself part of the developmental process, runs the risk of suffering in a similar way. In short, it is not possible to skip developmental stages without causing damage which may only appear in the future. A good example of this can be found in studies on the consequences of early independence in children (Modell 1975).

Freud's own account of his use of this sort of "blackmail" reveals results that fell short of what was intended, as the patients to whom it was applied, after an apparent initial success, later came to need re-analysis. Probably placing pressure of this sort on the analysand results from the analyst's wish to attain a certain goal that he sees as crucial to the analysis. With the attainment of this goal, the analytic process is brought to a close. The analyst has his own views about the end of the analysis, including those determined by the state of psychoanalytic knowledge at the time. (See the clinical examples given by Freud in his paper.) It therefore becomes difficult for him or her to face the possibility that the analysis has arrived at an impasse, but another analyst might be able to solve those problems not being dealt with by the present analyst. Ultimately, the difficulty for the analyst is having to face *his own* limitations with regard to a specific patient. He forces the analysis to end, not only because the patient's progress has stopped, but also because he does not want to acknowledge the narcissistic wound inflicted on him by the feeling of stagnation in the patient.

On Assessing Analytic "Terminability"

The concept of the end of an analysis is closely related to the medical concept of cure, which implies the total and absolute elimination of the disease and consequently of all pain. Psychoanalytically, if we applied such a concept, we would have to consider, among other things, symptom elimination, the overcoming of resistances, and making the unconscious conscious. Of course, such approaches to "cure" are always partial because they have little to say about the highly complex and dynamic aspects of the psyche.

At present we are not in a position to understand the complexities of the psyche any more than we are to understand the workings of other aspects of the organism. Thus we can aim at getting only limited results, whether through psychoanalysis or medicine in general. We also have to take into account the facts that the organism does not remain invariant over the course of time and that it is subjected to the action of pathogenic factors. So, for example, the individual who is treated once for an infection and cured does not have complete immunity against new infections. Similarly, the psyche undergoes changes following new (favorable or adverse) experiences, as well as changes due to maturation and aging. Even though an individual may be able to show greater ability to face and solve psychic conflicts, acquisition of absolute immunity to new psychopathological manifestations cannot be demanded as a condition of termination of analysis. It is not to be expected that "by means of analysis" we can either "attain to a level of absolute psychic normality" or "remain stable, as though, perhaps, we had succeeded in resolving every one of the patient's repressions and in filling in all the gaps in his memory" (pp. 219–20).

In his paper Freud discusses the various problems relating to termination and gives an account of two clinical cases (pp. 221–23). Although interesting, they are no longer appropriate for illustrating the problems of ending an analysis. The description given by Freud, especially in its reference to the extremely short length of the analyses, could today be used to illustrate the duration only of an analytically oriented psychotherapy which obtained good results. Such work would be considered an example of "brief psychotherapy," which can be structured either as of limited duration, that is, from six to twenty-five sessions (Small 1974), or without limits—open-ended therapy lasting from a few months to several years (Luborsky 1984). If we go by the accumulated knowledge and experience which we have at our disposal at present, we would not venture to analyze the "transference neurosis," much less the "negative transference"—so important in the first example given by Freud—in so short a time. Also, the severe problems of femininity and genitality shown in the second case would not be expected to be resolved in the transference in the time mentioned—at least not in a way that could enable the patient to face the anxieties of a hysterectomy without a recurrence of her illness. In spite of these considerations, it should be emphasized that Freud's thoughts about the termination of the analysis remain as valid now as at the time they were formulated.

The Constitutional Strength of the Instinct or Drive

Although instinctual forces are important and even fundamental pillars of psychoanalytic theory, their origin and nature have not yet been adequately clarified. It is accepted that in every animal species the instincts show specific characteristics, and all the evidence points to their hereditary nature, although some authors support the view that so-called instinctual behavior may also be learned.

The transmission of instincts by heredity implies the existence of instincts that belong to the species and that cannot be qualitatively altered in the course of an individual's life. But from a quantitative standpoint, the instincts can vary in the course of the developmental process. So, for example, a genital drive that is present in the individual at birth can be said to be a given feature of the developmental process, but at the same time it is capable of undergoing important enhancements following the hormonal changes of puberty. In aging, as well as in states of physical or mental exhaustion and in serious illnesses, the opposite may happen.

We may conclude that both Freud's conceptions are correct. There is a constitutional instinctual strength, as well as an instinctual strength "at the time" (p. 224). The strength of the instinct or drive is one of the fundamental factors to be considered in an analysis and in assessing the possibilities for change in regard to pathogenic conflicts. However, the picture is seen in its entirety only when we look at the instinctual forces in their relation to the ego. The ego of the human being is able, in order to develop and because of the complexity of its structure, not only to obtain adequate satisfaction, but also to delay it, suppress it, or even change it, making it unrecognizable at the time of its external manifestation.

The possibility of an instinct living in perfect and lasting harmony with the ego is utopian, since the instincts or drives may, depending on the situation, be accepted or rejected by the ego. The relationship of instinct to ego presents certain characteristics that are specific to each individual. For instance, the ego may deal with the instincts through the use of mechanisms of defense, and these are an integral part of the working and development of the ego of that person, determining his character (Moore and Fine 1968).

An analysis is unable to create new forms of functioning that are alien to the human being. Analysis, however, may assist the ego in helping the person to abandon the predominant use of primitive defenses (for example, massive projection) in favor of more developed and differentiated ones, making an attempt at a solution less pathogenic, although traces of the occasional use of primitive defenses may remain. This is why Freud arrived at the conclusion that it is not to be expected from an analysis that the relationships between the ego and the instincts will be different from those occurring "under favourable and normal conditions."

The Possibility of the Patient Being Protected against Further Psychic Conflict

The idea of prophylaxis against future pathogenic psychic conflicts contradicts the psychoanalytic concept of a dynamic unconscious, in which there is no past or future, but only the present. The dynamic aspects of the relation of id to ego are always active; consequently, psychic conflict is *always present*. In the course of the analytic process the development of the transference neurosis makes the conflict available for analysis, and it is the adequate analysis of this neurosis that permits insight, as well as the working through of the most important features of the psychic conflict as seen in the present. This in turn allows for a true prophylaxis in regard to further psychopathology. The possibility that later pathogenic conflicts may occur is, in our view, due to a failure to analyze certain crucial features that have remained hidden or that were not adequately perceived, examined, or resolved. The only way in which appropriate prophylaxis of pathogenic psychic conflicts can occur is as a consequence of consistent analysis of the scope, depth, and consistency of the transference.

Alterations in the Ego Structure

The person who begins analysis presents ego modifications that do not permit him a successful resolution of his psychic conflicts, despite his having a relatively normal or integrated ego, one which makes a therapeutic alliance with the analyst possible. Such ego alterations may be congenital or acquired in origin, and are due to the inadequacy of the defense mechanisms employed by the person. The specific mechanisms used will determine the characterological aspects of the individual and his predominant form of resistance toward the analytic process. Undoing the pathogenic defenses is the main task to be performed by the analysand, with the help of the analyst, and it is one of the factors determining the termination of the analysis (Fenichel 1945).

The difficulty faced in the work of overcoming resistances is related to the patient's fear of changes perceived as threats to the ego. Overcoming a resistance implies an alteration in the ego, as it involves a change in the defense mechanisms used against the instinctual threat. The likelihood of a change, or even of an alteration in the ego, is accompanied by a fear of the inefficiency of the new solution or of the new defensive procedure adopted to deal with fears that the ego may be overwhelmed by instinctual forces. This anxiety is due to an "incursion into the unknown" (Grinberg and Grinberg 1971). Fears of the sort described, experienced as a threat of a possible destruction of the ego, need gradual and thorough analytic work. Such work conveys a feeling of safety to the patient and prevents him feeling that he is being intruded upon by an analyst who demands quick solutions from him. In the course of the delicate task of understanding every detail of the resistances or of the defense mechanisms, the patient will experience small, steady, but also basic alterations in his ego. These constitute losses which require the continual work of mourning. When such changes continue to occur and are cumulative, the patient will slowly come to feel alterations occurring in himself, and this may lead to a perception of change in his identity as a whole. The changes in the resistances, the alterations of the ego, and the possibility of change in the deployment of instinctual forces, all attained without major anxieties, determine important transformations in the relationship between the individual and his internal and external objects. In particular, the modification of the connection between the individual and his internal objects brings about change in the characteristics of those objects.

Origin of the Structural Variations in the Ego

The forces originating in the id are those that most influence and determine the characteristics of the ego. This is due both to the peculiarities of the id and to its links with the ego. For example, the drives arising from the id—Eros, as well as Thanatos—need to be mentally represented in the ego, in the form of fantasy, in order to gain a psychic manifestation. The variety of ways in which Eros and Thanatos can combine or oppose each other will determine the internal richness of the individual, which will be expressed in his fantasy life. The way in which the ego deals with such drive combinations will define the creativity of the individual's inner world and its derivatives—including behavior, actions, symptoms, affects, and many other manifestations. It will also determine his mechanisms of defense (p. 246).

It is possible that the characteristics described by Freud as the "mobility" or "adhesiveness" of the libido (p. 241) are due not to some peculiarity of the drive itself, but rather to the way in which the ego deals with the conflicts originating from the drives. Both drive adhesiveness and mobility reflect defense against loss of part of the ego and an object. Where adhesiveness is operative, the change implies the loss of a type of defense and of an object. Mobility reflects a state where neither the object nor the alterations within the ego matter, as neither is permanent.

By way of an example, we shall describe a young female patient who came into analysis prompted by an inner incompatibility between her femininity and her profession, which she felt was a masculine activity. The patient imagined that in order to keep her marriage and her children she could not have a professional life—especially not the competent and successful one she had the capacity to have. She believed that if she were to function successfully as a professional, she would lose her husband and her children and would in effect become a man—since she would lose her maternal identifications—or even her own mother. Such fantasied losses were an impediment to the inner reorganization of her feminine identifications and her internal relationships to her mother and her profession.

Nothing we have considered clarifies or explains the variability of ego structure or of instinctual manifestations. This is a difficult and complex field of study and remains obscure. We may ask what is the importance in this context of inherited and acquired factors, as mentioned by Freud in his paper. The difficulty lies, it seems, in identifying and separating the two in any given person, particularly because there is an interplay between these sets of factors from birth, possibly from conception. This difficulty also emerges when one tries to determine the origin of the ego and of the id. Although Freud considered the ego to be derived from the id, he remarked that "even before the ego has come into existence, the lines of development, trends and reactions which it will later exhibit are already laid down for it" (p. 240). This point of view implies that he conceived of the ego as partially inherited and independent from the id in its origin, as well as having the potential for those structural characteristics which will develop later.

It is possible that this suggestion of Freud gave rise to the important school of ego psychology, which stresses, among many other concepts, the existence of an "autonomous" and "conflict-free" part of the ego. Quantitative studies are currently being undertaken by researchers who are trying to identify which factor—the inherited or the environmental—is predominant in neurosis and psychosis. These researches obviously imply a search for the cause of those alterations in ego structure that allow a psychopathology to emerge, but they have not yet proved conclusive. Studies of biochemical disturbances in neuronal transmission in families which have a schizophrenic or manic-depressive psychotic member suggest the great importance of heredity as a dominant factor in the emergence of such psychoses and consequently in the ego structures characteristic of such persons (Rainer 1985).

We have pointed out that the defense mechanisms determine an individual's personality type, his character, and the way he deals with the anxieties arising from his psychic conflicts. Thus the defense mechanisms determine some of the most important aspects of the individual's ego structure. We may ask how these mechanisms are selected. Is it possible that a traumatic childhood situation determines the selection of a given mechanism? Or is the selection caused by recurring dominant situations in the person's life? Or by the type of conflict? Can they be due to heredity, or are they a result of identification with persons in the environment, particularly the mother? We can ask, for example, whether a mother who handles her anxieties by isolating herself from other people will teach her child the same kind of response to his or her own anxieties. We can also think of the mother who, faced with her baby's discomfort or distress, fills him with food and leads him to believe that eating solves everything.

In conclusion, we could say that much has been discussed and investigated regarding the formation of ego structure, but many areas of knowledge remain to be clarified—areas such as the development of the mother-child link and its role in determining the characteristics of the future ego (Joseph 1973).

The Personality of the Analyst

In section VII Freud discusses the training analysis in a way that does not correspond to our current thinking on the subject. He says that the training analysis is no more than a learning procedure aimed at enabling the future analyst to identify the nature of the unconscious and to perceive his patient's unconscious. Although such goals are very desirable, they certainly cannot be attained in the training analyses that Freud had in mind in "Analysis Terminable and Interminable." It is doubtful, to say the least, that a three-week psychotherapy, followed by another lasting two more weeks, would enable someone to recognize the existence of his unconscious. It is also worth asking whether a patient who has no natural and spontaneous perception of his unconscious can develop the capacity for insight needed for future work as an analyst by means of his personal analysis alone (Etchegoyen 1987). Such limitations imply that the would-be analyst could never reach the goal of changing his own analysis from "a terminable into an interminable task" (p. 249), as we rely on the fact that the processes begun in his own analysis do not cease when it ends. We also rely on the fact that the reshaping of the ego proceeds spontaneously in the analyzed individual and that he makes use of all his subsequent experiences in this newly acquired sense. Freud concludes that this "makes the analysed subject qualified to be an analyst himself" (p. 249). It is well known that the training analysis has become more complex and ambitious, both for the training analyst and for the would-be analyst. The standard analysis of a patient has simpler and more modest goals (Blecourt 1973).

The profession of analyst is exceedingly demanding, for it can at any time threaten the structure of the analyst's own personality. In his analytic activity he is bound to face the neurotic and psychotic anxieties of the analysand, and these anxieties will call into action, to variable extent and depth, his own corresponding anxieties. For this reason he should be prepared to rein in such anxieties and not to let himself be overwhelmed by them, as well as to use his perception for a better understanding and interpretation of his patient (Etchegoyen 1987). Analysts, both in the past and in the present, have become ill through not having been able to enjoy the prophylactic benefits of an analysis (incorrectly called a training or didactic analysis) carried out to an extent and depth that enables them to maintain ego integrity in the face of their difficult ongoing analytic work (Gitelson 1983). Could this be the reason why so many of Freud's early disciples and followers became seriously ill? Freud's recommendation of a reanalysis every five years or so could have been made with a view to avoiding such problems. Another reason for reanalysis is to forestall the possible deterioration of the analyst, both personally and professionally, with consequences that may be harmful to his patients and to himself. Through reanalysis he could try to regain temporarily lost abilities and avoid relapse.

In general, reanalysis is a procedure that the analyst finds it difficult to accept. When he does accept it, it is not an easy job to undertake, partly owing to narcissistic features in the analysand and partly because the peculiarities of the analytic milieu present the would-be reanalysand with problems such as the limited availability of analysts for the task, the rivalry between analysts, and threats to the professional status of the reanalysand.

The Analyst's Repudiation of Femininity

Freud thought that one of the most serious problems faced by the analyst in his work is the repudiation of femininity, in men as well as in women. The man rejects his passivity and the woman her lack of a penis. Freud thought that the resolution was accomplished in both cases by repression. He believed that the man's passivity and the woman's wish to have a penis were difficult to identify and to deal with in analysis. The obstacle in the woman's analysis is due to the impossibility of renouncing the wish for a penis, with which the analysis cannot provide her. We can see these problems in the analyses described by Freud. However, there are other important problems relating to all the factors that influence the fate of adult sexuality (see Blum 1977).

Both men and women are naturally bound, from early infancy, to have both masculine and feminine identifications, and their egos acquire characteristics from both parents. Castration anxiety alone cannot determine the predominance of sexual identification with the parent of the same sex in adolescence, for hereditary factors which operate even before birth are also present, determining biological, anatomical, and hormonal characteristics (Galenson and Roiphe 1977).

It is possible that both males and females have some unconscious knowledge of the anatomical configuration of their genitals, the male being aware that his penis is destined to penetrate and the female that her vagina has an emptiness to be filled. It may be thought that an innate knowledge of our body precedes our objective knowledge. If this is correct—and everything points to it—there is an urge in the individual to perform the specific function linked with his or her genital organs. The sensations connected with this will also determine the body-ego characteristics (Kleeman 1977). In adolescence the changes in hormonal balance activate the sexual drives intensively in both sexes, increasing the male's wish to penetrate and the female's to be penetrated. The attainment of these objectives implies the boy's renunciation of feminine wishes and the girl's giving up the wish for a penis. That the parent of the same sex has the identical anatomical configuration is a facilitating factor in bringing about the repression of those drives that characterize the opposite sex.

Considering that both males and females have the mother as their first object of envy, one may ask: What is the importance of this fact in the development, establishment, and consolidation of masculine and feminine identity? What is its influence in establishing the characteristics of the relationships formed by adult men and women? Would envy of the breast determine the form of the man-woman collusion in giving the man primacy in the relationship of the couple? Does the early envy a boy feels for his mother lead him to long for femininity and the ability to bear children?

FINAL REMARKS

When Freud wrote "Analysis Terminable and Interminable" he tried to look at analysis realistically. He wanted to examine the possibilities and limitations of his method, as well as those characteristics of the analysand and the analyst which impose restrictions on the duration, termination, and results of analysis.

It is possible that when Freud studied the problem of the length of analysis and the attempts made to shorten it, he did not fully take into consideration the importance of the fact that analysis is a process and, as such, goes through a number of stages. These stages must be passed through naturally, and they are determined by the psychic characteristics of the patient, as well as by the way he and his analyst interrelate. This is due to the fact that the analytic process has to be inserted into the developmental process of the individual. The analytic process then becomes part of the more general developmental one.

What are the consequences of the intertwining of these two processes — the developmental and the analytic — for the patient? When they interact, the analytic process will bring about slow and progressive changes in the analysand's development. In such a case, evaluation of the length of analysis changes substantially, for it depends on the duration and progression of the developmental process. This means that the analysis, as a process, is interminable.

It is likely that one can talk about termination of the analysis when the analysand can tolerate the main changes inherent in the developmental process. Principal among these is the development of an adequate capacity for separation and autonomy in relation to the analyst. Such autonomy and separation imply that the patient is able to face substantial changes in his identity, in his ego — including his body ego, and in his internal and external objects. On the other hand, to ask analysis to make alterations that can prevent new conflicts from arising, or even to prevent the revival of those that brought the patient into analysis in the first place, is to ask it to change, in a most radical way, the person's nature, history, and scars from his past and present natural limitations. The foregoing remarks must also refer to the training analysis, as the analyst-to-be must make his own analysis interminable for a number of reasons. He faces the difficult task of having continually to visualize the patient's unconscious as well as his own. More precisely, he has to be aware of the peculiarities of the interplay between his unconscious and that of his patient. The adequate perception of this interplay has, as a consequence, the result that the analyst will constantly have new perceptions of his or her own self, and so can increase and deepen an understanding of the patient. However, this task presents many difficulties. The main one is the requirement to be aware of his or her own limitations as a person and as a psychoanalyst, without needing to deny such limitations. Implicit in this process is the disruption of the analyst's omnipotent evaluation of those personal concepts and practices that he or she considers to be good psychoanalytic technique. Such a disturbance may cause the analyst to experience the loss of aspects of self, but if this loss is negotiated successfully, a new understanding of self, as well as of the patient, is substituted.

When the analyst becomes aware that the difficulties involved in facing one's own personal problems, as well as those of the patient, are too great to deal with satisfactorily, then we have an indication that the analyst needs to continue or to begin a new analysis.

Freud's personal situation—old age, illness, the loss of important objects, as well as the Nazi persecution of both Jews and psychoanalysis—certainly influenced his last contributions. In this essay we have discussed the eight problems he examined in "Analysis Terminable and Interminable," with conclusions as follows:

1. Separation anxiety in the patient and his fantasy of loss of infantile gratification are important factors in a lengthy analysis. At times these factors may be observed in the analyst, who, as a reaction to such fantasies and limitations, may brusquely shorten or end the analysis.

2. We take the view that analysis is an interminable process because it becomes a part of the analysand's life. Its end marks only a particular moment in a developmental process, a moment determined by a mutually agreed interruption of meetings between analyst and analysand.

3. Freud's views on the constitutional strength of drives are appropriate, for they take into account all the variations in his theoretical approach, although there are inevitably gaps in our understanding.

4. The most effective preventive measure against future psychic conflict is an adequate analysis of the transference. However, this security is relative, for human beings have limitations determined by their personalities, by their pasts, and by the vicissitudes of their futures which can arouse a past pathology or cause a new one to emerge.

5. The mechanisms of defense are the main obstacles to the progress of the analysis because of the fear linked with overcoming resistance, a process that implies a change in the ego and a new way of dealing with a drive. This alteration causes a loss of part of the ego as well as a fear that the new way of dealing with the drive may be inefficient, threatening the ego with destruction.

6. The origins of structural variations in the ego are still obscure, in spite of constant research, because of difficulties in evaluating the relative impor-

tance of inherited and environmental factors. The defense mechanisms, which are part of the ego structure, may have acquired characteristics from hereditary factors as well as from the specific mother-child interaction.

7. The future analyst must have a capacity for spontaneous insight and must be sufficiently well analyzed to be able to develop characteristics appropriate to his or her function as an analyst. These are necessary in order to tolerate reformulations in self understanding, as well as understanding of the patient. In addition, each analyst needs to have a perception of his or her personal and technical limitations.

8. There are obstacles arising in the analysis from penis envy and from castration anxiety in both sexes, but conflicts related to the first object relationships and to the envy of the breast should also be considered. In determining gender identity, hereditary and hormonal factors play a part, and the unconscious perception of one's own genital configuration and sexual destiny are factors that must be added to those already cited.

REFERENCES

Blecourt, A., de. 1973. Similarities and differences between analysis and therapeutic analysis. In *Psychoanalytic training in Europe: 10 years of discussion*. Barcelona: European Psycho-Analytical Federation Bulletin Monographs, 1983.

Blum, H. 1977. *Female psychology*. New York: International Universities Press.

Etchegoyen, R. H. 1987. *Fundamentos da técnica psicanalítica*. Porto Alegre: Artes Médicas.

Fenichel, O. 1945. *The psychoanalytic theory of neurosis*. New York: W. W. Norton.

Gaburri, G. 1985. On termination of the analysis. *Int. Rev. Psycho-Anal.* 12:461.

Galenson, E., and Roiphe, H. 1977. Some suggested revisions concerning early female development. In *Female psychology*, by H. Blum. New York: International Universities Press, 1977.

Gitelson, F. H. 1983. Identity crises: Splits or compromise—adaptive or maladaptive. In *The identity of the psychoanalyst*. Edited by E. D. Joseph and D. Widlöcher. New York: International Universities Press.

Glover, E. 1955. *The technique of psycho-analysis*. London: Baillière, Tindall and Cox.

Grinberg, L., and Grinberg, R. 1971. *Identidad y cambio*. Buenos Aires: Editiones Kargieman.

Grotjahn, M. 1966. Karl Abraham, 1875–1925: The first German psychoanalyst. In *Psychoanalytic pioneers*. Edited by F. Alexander et al. New York: Basic Books.

92 / David Zimmermann and A. L. Bento Mostardeiro

Jones, E. 1957. *Sigmund Freud: Life and work*, Volume 3. London: Hogarth.

Joseph, E. 1973. Psicanálise—Ciência, pesquisa e estudo de gêmeos. *Rev. Brasileira de Psicanálise* 9:83–114.

Kleeman, J. A. 1977. Freud's views on early female sexuality in the light of direct child observation. In *Female Psychology*, by H. Blum. New York: International Universities Press, 1977.

Lorand, S. 1966. Sándor Ferenczi, 1873–1933: Pioneer of pioneers. In *Psychoanalytic pioneers*. Edited by F. Alexander et al. New York: Basic Books.

Luborsky, L. 1984. *Principles of psychoanalytic psychotherapy: A manual for supportive-expressive treatment*. New York: Basic Books.

Modell, A. 1975. A narcissistic defence against affects and the illusion of self-sufficiency. *Int. J. Psycho-Anal.* 56:275–82.

Moore, B., and Fine, B. 1968. *A glossary of psychoanalytic terms and concepts*. New York: American Psychoanalytic Association.

Rainer, J. 1985. Genetics and psychiatry. In *Comprehensive textbook of psychiatry*. Edited by H. Kaplan and B. Saddock. Volume 1. Baltimore and London: William and Wilkins.

Robert, M. 1964. *The psychoanalytic revolution*. London: Allen and Unwin, 1967.

Small, L. 1974. *As psicoterapias breves*. Rio de Janeiro: Imago Editora.

Obstacles to
Analytic Cure

TERTTU ESKELINEN DE FOLCH

". . . the question should be asked of what are the obstacles
that stand in the way of such a cure."
FREUD, "Analysis Terminable and Interminable"

Fifty years after the publication of "Analysis Terminable and Interminable"
we are still questioning some of the problems encountered in psychoanalytic
therapy that had been a source of concern to Freud. Some of our patients,
having progressed resolutely, revert to their old ways of dealing with conflict;
others appear to derive more satisfaction from the painful repetition of
impaired relationships than from embarking on new and positive ones. Others, in spite of many years of treatment, seem to become hopelessly entangled
in external situations instead of applying and committing themselves to the
work of analysis in order "to salvage from the whirlpool of their own feelings the deepest truths" (Freud 1930, p. 133).

Can we now usefully supplement Freud's explanation of the clinical facts
that induced him to write "Analysis Terminable and Interminable"? We now
treat patients who would in the past not have been accepted for analysis, and
we have seen the development of analytic technique, including the more
consistent and effective analysis of the interaction between the analytic couple (the here-and-now of the transference–countertransference).

It may be argued that our present-day explanatory capacity is still not
sufficient to alter the handling and resolution of the problems considered by

Freud. However, I believe that we *are* now in a position to attempt new explanations of the old problems in view of the wealth of clinical experience accumulated in the last few decades and the theoretical and technical advances accruing from the contributions of several generations of analysts. While these explanations neither confirm nor drastically modify Freud's original ideas, they nevertheless expand the links between clinical difficulty, variations in technical orientation, and the use we may make of metapsychological and theoretical principles in the statement of the problem in its present form (for example, the structure of the unconscious, the fusion of instincts and their vicissitudes, and archaic forms of mental processes).

In this chapter I shall try to focus on some of these links, with a view to illuminating the points of correspondence between particular incidents, whether active or closed off, in our present-day psychoanalytic practice and plausible explanations of the obscure points which Freud, in such an exemplary manner, induced us to try to clarify. With regard to the clinical facts mentioned at the beginning of this chapter, I shall confine myself to two topics:

1. *The problem of the analyzability of certain nuclei of the personality that appear to be remote from the analytic relationship and analytic experience*, which I shall call *concealed nuclei of the personality*. In view of the difficulties in extracting them from their marginal position and bringing them into the light of a shared experience in the analytic session, it is legitimate to enquire—to enquire again after Freud —about particular features of the repetition compulsion which so bewilderingly and stubbornly oppose any change.

2. *Technical problems.*

CONCEALED NUCLEI OF THE PERSONALITY

Freud comments in his paper on the difficulties of handling the negative transference if this is intentionally aroused or provoked by the analyst. He describes the powerful resistances presented by the patient to admitting to consciousness the unacceptable, disturbing impulses and the associated memories. However, Freud considers that, in order for the ego to be capable of functioning satisfactorily, the analysis must integrate the disparate impulses sufficiently. They must be "tamed" by all the "trends of the ego" and dominated by libido. Freud's major concern here appears to be with the negative aspects of feelings and impulses, rather than with binding the positive aspects. These negative aspects had occupied him as early as 1912 ("On the Universal Tendency to Debasement in the Sphere of Love"), when he spoke of "something in the nature of the sexual instinct itself [that] is unfavourable to the realization of complete satisfaction" (pp. 188–89). Later (Freud 1920), he was to refer to these aspects as the death instinct.

In our relations with some of our patients, we observe the difficulties they have in confronting destructive impulses, hatred or envy. Even after a long period of analysis, it is difficult for them to acknowledge these feelings as belonging to them. It is as if they feel that the integrity of their personalities would be threatened if they were to experience, even for an instant, the reactivation of these destructive impulses or feelings. They use all kinds of defenses to avoid such consciousness, feeling at the same time exposed to the potential risk of losing their mental balance.

We see that such patients live under the threat of something terrifying and potentially destructive of their integrity. Melanie Klein described a panicky fear of very primitive, terrifying objects which have been thrust away into the distance. They have been dispatched to unconscious levels deeper than those in which other, less terrifying objects are accommodated. After rejection by the superego and the ego, they appear to be particularly inaccessible to any form of integration and hence to analytic work. Melanie Klein assumes that the analyst comes into contact with this situation in confronting resistance from the ego and the superego. In my opinion, there is also a resistance from the id, resulting from the nature of the objects I shall now describe.

The relevant technical problem can be formulated as follows: Do these split-off objects, with their corresponding affects and impulses relegated to the deepest unconscious levels, appear only during a crisis in the observable behavior of an individual? Can we not have any contact with these objects in less extreme situations?

In my view, these objects *are* present in the object relation and hence in the relationship with the analyst. They are present in the specific way in which the individual uses splitting or dissociation, both as a mental mechanism and as the expression of an impulse. The more destructive and terrifying these archaic objects are, the more such patients disconnect or fragment ideas in a destructive and annihilating fashion. I shall illustrate this by a brief case history concerning a highly schizoid patient who did not present any clinical signs of psychosis.

Mr. X is a middle-aged intellectual who, despite a brilliant academic career and a stable family situation, feels that he is not living authentically, that something vital is lacking in his relationship with his wife, and that he lives with the threat of disaster. He seems to be appreciated by his colleagues and students and speaks of both with warm interest. He also appears capable of critical judgment in his university department. With his analyst, he is at first positive but soon falls silent, declaring that he has nothing to say. After a few months of analysis he begins to dream of terrorists and people who set fire to bookshops. At times he is the terrorist in his dreams, yet he maintains that they have nothing to do with him and attributes them to his reading of modern terror stories.

At the beginning of his analysis he dreams something that later becomes significant. A small boy is playing on a balcony, from which he is in danger of falling. Mr. X then sees himself in a diver's suit taking a shower, and becomes excited. In a third part of the same dream, he is carrying his own dead body, which he presents to a woman—the small boy's mother—asking her to draw up his death certificate, the cause of death being something like "death by annihilation."

I shall not go into the excitement involved in all this. For the time being, I want to consider only how this dream relates to the way Mr. X manages to cut off, dissociate, deaden, and ultimately annihilate important parts of his personality. His relationship with me showed how all this was connected with the object. He seemed to drop any interpretation I gave him and to avoid any vital, spontaneous response to my interpretations, taking refuge in schizoid aloofness. Sometimes, after a silence, he would come up with equally dead and abstract generalizations. On one level, he was dissociating his own mind and reactions, but at the same time he was devitalizing the relationship with me. I came to think that his terrifying object appeared constantly and actively in our usual relationship in the form of ideas and feelings which annihilated any vital bond between us. For this reason, his responses to my interpretations lacked life. In the following session all this was expressed quite openly.

One Monday the patient expressed much more intense anxiety than usual. He said he had a pain in his chest that he thought might herald a heart attack. Very unusually for him, he said he had felt immense rage against me when he had realized that we might speak of important things. When he arrived the next day he said that, for the first time, he could see the possibility of a way out of the vicious circle in which he felt himself to be. But he added that something strange had happened to him in the lift on the way to the session. A sign reading EXIT was stuck on one door, while the other door seemed to open into the void. A sudden thought had passed through his mind: "What if I were to go through the door to the precipice!" When we discussed this idea—his move toward the precipice—we could relate it to his way of plunging into silence after those moments when he seemed to have achieved some true contact. The patient expressed horror at the thought that his image of himself as a warm and understanding person was not at all accurate. He remained silent for some ten minutes. I also said nothing, waiting for him to come out of his closed-in state of his own accord after showing that he was able to contemplate his attitude more openly than usual. What in fact happened was that he spoke of his silence and expressed his surprise that he could be indifferent to it. He had even felt a certain excitement and delight. He looked at his watch and saw that only two minutes remained in the session. Well, he said, he had forgotten to tell me that he and his wife had finally decided to have a child—they had been discussing it for the past few days. He had also had a dream that was different from his usual dreams. He was at the seaside with his wife. There was a boy, perhaps it was his son . . . There was also a very large family, friends of his parents, whom he had known since childhood. He got on well with them all and had played with those children many times . . .

All this had been about to be consigned to oblivion, to fall from a "precipice" with his silence. And this happened after he had glimpsed a way out of his vicious circle and had had an inkling of warmer, more affectionate feelings toward me as a parent figure! He had apparently felt this for some time and, thanks to his identification with me, dared to imagine himself as a father having a son. He probably felt more secure now and capable of accepting some of the most unpleasant and rejected parts of himself. In other words, he could confront more things directly and tell me of his enjoyment at seeing me powerless to help him. In attacks of this kind, where envy appears so clearly as a motive, it would be interesting to clarify whether the patient acts out in identification with those sinister objects isolated in his deep unconscious that are so difficult to reintegrate.

A number of theoretical implications can be considered from the point of view of the correspondence between instincts, ego structure, and object relations. For example:

1. Highly destructive defense mechanisms such as splitting are fueled by the death instinct, whose nature and strength they express.
2. The processes of splitting are related to objects, both internal and external,

and to the analyst in the analysis. It is the analyst's interpretation that is rejected and excluded, as well as the result of this interpretation (in the case of Mr. X, his ability to trust and the plan to have a child). This can be observed in the analysis. But what may become comprehensible to the analyst may become accessible to the patient's experience only after a prolonged period of work. This will happen when he acknowledges these impulses as his own, but it may follow that

3. The patient finds himself caught in the repetition of the sinister, painful experience and may derive satisfaction from it. This is a type of sado-masochistic satisfaction that appears to have a life of its own, quite independent of the trends of the ego. Often the patient strongly resists giving it up.

With regard to these matters, I should like to mention a difficulty for analysis which in my opinion results from a particular form of repetition compulsion connected with concealed nuclei of the personality, a difficulty to which Bion referred in connection with bizarre objects (Bion 1957;1958). Bion tells us that, in order to get rid of intolerable emotions, the individual fragments his objects and expels them from his self. These fragments then engulf or are engulfed by external objects, which become greatly distorted and persecutory. The individual then feels threatened by these objects, which invade him—for example, in the form of hallucination. Even if not clinically psychotic, patients, whether adults or children, who have important psychotic areas in their personalities feel compelled to make pacts with these bizarre objects. These pacts have a greater or lesser degree of organization and are eventually erotized. Such patients feel not so much persecuted as caught up in compulsive acting out. They are locked into a vicious circle by virtue of the intensity of the death drive and resultant envious attacks. When the analyst succeeds in making real contact with such patients and their anxieties—always a difficult process—their envy is exacerbated and consequently so is compulsive repetition.

A four-year-old boy in analysis alternated between virtual hallucination (fear of dust particles) and compulsive and excited acting out. When he came into contact with intolerable feelings—jealousy, aggressive fantasies, and guilt feelings—Alberto broke the toys that represented his objects, in particular his brother, and threw them into an empty space bounded by the table, the wall, and a cupboard. This empty space afterward seemed to have an uncanny attraction for him, as well as arousing terror. He began to fall down in it deliberately and compulsively, while full of excitation. This was repeated in a number of sessions, alternating with terror of dust, which he sometimes believed rushed at him threateningly. The empty space appeared to become the representative of an object which seemed to grab fragmented pieces of him. This internal situation was repeated with me. He would arrive screaming, so that I would have to take him in my arms and carry him into the consulting room. I noticed that his expression often showed the same mixture of terror and excitation as when he fell down in the empty space. Sometimes he gave up and fell asleep.

Alberto's two attitudes of terror and excitement helped me to understand the strange links the boy was forging through his compulsive actions and also to understand how he used them to avoid a much more terrifying hallucinatory state. Alberto showed me that he was excitedly repeating the fate of his objects when he allowed himself to fall and be, as it were, engulfed by them, as if he wanted to pacify them and the new bizarre objects he had produced. I believe that many patients who compulsively repeat more or less strange actions are using this repetition to try to keep more terrifying objects at bay, deploying constant measures to placate them.

Since these objects, which are the result of a violent split, invade the external object which is subsequently introjected, they threaten terrifyingly to invade, mutilate, and capture the subject. The extent of this process will depend on the degree to which a part of the personality has been able to develop normally and establish other object relations. If this normal facet is not sufficient, clinical psychosis will result. It seems to me that many of these perverse compulsive repetitions are connected with this more or less normal part of the personality, which is desperately struggling with psychotic anxiety. It is difficult to bring it into harmony with other trends in the ego and it has its own automatic ways of obtaining satisfaction (p. 225). It is not the strength of the life instinct and its psychic representative, love, which shapes this independent way to satisfaction described by Freud, but the strength of the destructive impulse. Love would represent the integrating strength of the individual searching for an object.

I have used the example of these two patients to describe serious hindrances to the analytic cure. I have also tried to show how Melanie Klein's theory of the anxieties and defensive organizations of the paranoid-schizoid position gives us a broader understanding of those nuclei which used to appear beyond the reach of analysis and also enables us to make better contact with them in the analytic relationship. The possibility of changing the fate of these object relations, which is conditioned by the anxieties and defensive organizations mentioned above, will depend on the violence of the splitting processes and hence on the state of fragmentation of the self and of the objects. It will also depend on the amount of excitation and satisfaction derived by the patient from this situation.

We can imagine the types of relationship these patients form with the outside world from the way they use their analysts. For example, four-year-old Alberto allowed himself to be tied to a tree in the school playground and to be ill-treated by his schoolfellows. His intrapsychic world was dramatized in external reality. But, unlike the analyst, the people around him respond to his manner and influence the style of the dramatization of acting out. Some of them are caught up in the action, so that they fall in with the acting out. Such situations give rise to extremely difficult family relationships, causing suffering to child and parents alike.

Melanie Klein's concept of projective identification (1946) has helped us to understand a person's relations with the outside world, not only in these severe cases, but also in less serious ones. It gives us, additionally, a broader understanding of the patient who is locked into the paranoid-schizoid position in his relationship with the analyst.

TECHNICAL PROBLEMS

When a person has recourse principally to splitting and projective identification, his intrapsychic conflict becomes a conflict in external reality—an interpersonal conflict. Put in such concise form, this is an oversimplification. In fact, both splitting and repression operate simultaneously in such a way that some parts of the internal conflict may remain repressed while other parts undergo splitting and projection. We may say that the more archaic the objects and the intolerable feelings, the more they will be dealt with by splitting and by projection onto people around the patient. Betty Joseph (1983) and other authors (including Bott-Spillius 1983) have written at length on the technical problems of analyzing a patient locked into the paranoid-schizoid position, with a view to understanding the relationship established with the analyst through acting out.

The verbal and nonverbal communications of these patients are understood as ways of projecting and then of dealing with the parts projected onto the personality of the analyst. They take the place of conveying the patient's

concerns and his affect directly. Instead of communicating in a straightforward fashion, the patient tries to influence the analyst and to provoke reactions in him. He tries to get the analyst to act out some part or other of his
internal world. From this point of view, the analyst ceases to be a distant
observer and must instead be prepared to experience the reactions provoked
or evoked in him, and because of this to take more notice of his emotional
responses to the patient than in the past. More emphasis therefore comes to
be placed on the interaction in the sessions. Just as Freud originally considered the transference to be an obstacle to analysis, whereas it later became
the principal instrument, so it is today with the analyst's countertransference
responses and even his momentary collusion with patients, which we have
in the past considered to be serious obstacles to the progress of the treatment. Today we can regard the analyst's introspection into his countertransference reactions and his understanding of certain momentary collusions as
important factors in his comprehension of the patient's psychic world.

If we believe that the patient transfers his pathological object relations onto
the analytic relationship, it becomes unnecessary "to stir up a conflict which is
not at the time manifest" (p. 230). We have tried to show that unpleasant and
unbearable aspects of the personality penetrate into the analytic relationship
in one way or another even if they are split off and removed to a distance by
defense. The analyst can then bring them to the surface and cause them to be
experienced at the level on which the patient is enacting them (Malcolm 1986).

Nowadays we would say that the patient's ego is weakened by the massive
projection of parts of his objects and of his self onto the outside world, and
that one of the analyst's tasks is to help the patient to integrate these projected parts into his personality, to enable him to become capable of coping
with his own conflicts. It follows that the analyst's capacity to allow himself
to be affected by and to experience feelings that the patient is incapable of
assuming, and projects onto and evokes in him, as well as his ability to
verbalize these feelings and turn them into an experience shared with the
patient, can help the patient feel secure enough to experience them for himself. This presupposes that the patient has introjected an analyst capable of
confronting and considering that which is most intolerable, uncanny, or malignant. The analyst's task, however, is not easy. He does not speak from a
distance. His own emotional reactions may be aroused by the patient's pro-
jections, and sometimes the threat of an unpleasant relationship, or even a
veritable hell, may entangle him in the patient's defensive system so that the
emotional experience has to be kept at bay.

In "Negative Transference: From Split towards Integration" (1987) Pere Folch and I discuss the importance of this integration and describe some of the problems the analyst encounters on the way to its achievement. The diagram reproduced below may help to illustrate our points. Two vicious circles may hold up the process of integration. One is created by the analyst's collusion with the patient and the other by the patient's envy reactivated by the analyst's good interpretations and understanding.

Collusion of the Analyst

As stated earlier, if the analyst can, through his understanding, avoid the acting out in which the patient is trying to involve him, he has at his disposal an important instrument for clarifying the patient's intrapsychic functioning and helping him to reintegrate the parts previously projected. But the ana-

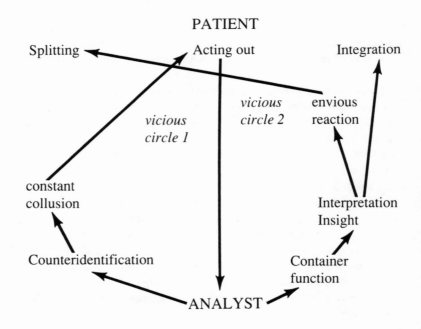

lyst may be caught up in situations with which he cannot cope and may then act out what the patient provokes in him or projects onto him, thus intensifying the split. For instance, a little girl in analytic treatment, seized with intense jealousy, could not tolerate the idea that I might have a sexual life when she was not with me. She had drawn a picture of some children looking on in fury at a situation which appeared to represent a copulating couple. She then insistently tried to get me to erase every indication of sex in the drawing and drew some pathetic tears on the faces of the children. This confronted me with a difficult choice. In effect she was saying, "You must choose. Something has to be rubbed out—either the children or the couple having sex." Faced with the dilemma of the pathetic tears or of losing my patient (her parents live apart, a fact which the little girl uses by threatening to abandon one and live with the other), I had to erase any idea of a couple or of sex which I might enjoy. A few moments later she asked me to fill in a drawing representing a decorative sphere from a Christmas tree. I had to fill in the sphere with small circles. Apparently she wanted to entice me into a sweet and beautiful Christmas fantasy in order to get rid of all her upset feelings at imagining me as a member of a couple, a thought which had disturbed her in the extreme.

Children clearly express their attempts to induce analysts and parents to collude with them, and they use various styles of coercion (tears, threats of abandonment, promises of good behavior and obedience, and the like). In the analysis of both adults and children, we can in fact make use of a whole range of "reasonable" arguments to avoid what is most difficult to confront in our dealings with patients. We may tell ourselves that the child is too fragile to look the truth in the face, that it is better to construct a stronger ego first, that it is preferable to build up a more solid transference relationship before interpreting the negative feelings, and so forth.

The analyst's way of colluding with his patient's defenses are as multiple and varied as are the structures of the personality. On the other hand, the form of the collusion may be very "analytic." Interpretation of conflicts expressed in events outside the transference or ones that have occurred in the patient's past may become one form of collusion. Keeping silent about the most disturbing point, constructing intellectual speculations, or allowing oneself to be carried away by the enthusiasm of a new discovery can disguise the disturbance experienced by the patient or the analyst.

The Patient's Envy

The second vicious circle, involving the patient's envy, is the most difficult obstacle to progress in the analysis. When it occurs the patient can tolerate only a misled analyst and an impoverished analysis. This is because his envy would be exacerbated by contact with an efficient and vital analyst. In section VI of his paper, Freud points out that the way some patients cling to illness and suffering goes far beyond the conflict between the ego and the superego. It is at this point that Freud links masochism, the negative therapeutic reaction, and the sense of guilt to the death instinct ("unmistakable indications of the presence of a power in mental life which we call the instinct of aggression or of destruction according to its aims" [p. 243]). In clinical practice, it is the envious reactions (as psychic representatives of the death instinct), produced when better and more hopeful relations arise, that impede progress and plunge the patient back into repetitive acting out. These patients very often maintain a kind of balance between hope and despair, which they have become accustomed to tolerate, but they are frightened by any clear progress, which would exacerbate their uncontrollable envy. Thus the analysis may stagnate.

We have considered two factors—namely, concealed nuclei of the personality, which emerge in vague and often unsuspected form in the analysis, and the forms of alienation of the personality in external reality, as referred to by Freud and nowadays clarified by increasingly detailed knowledge of the various forms of projective identification. These factors invite us to consider how best to apply the theses put forward in "Analysis Terminable and Interminable" to the creation of theoretical foundations for the clinical facts which today's techniques enable us to bring to light. Through them, and through explorations of the transference, we can recover the object relationship that exists behind the more or less severe fragmentation of the self and objects.

The theory of the death instinct and the repetition compulsion can help us today in building theory. The basic "disconnecting" character of the death instinct would be expressed in the implementation of splits, while highly primitive forms of the integrative character of the life instinct would act as a counterpoint in the dynamic of projective identification. Isolation of the self and accommodation of the fragments in a receiving object (internal or external) could be seen as both the cause and the effect of the catastrophic disorganization of the incipient psychical reality.

In our clinical work, what we call concealed nuclei of the personality may appear as the most sinister result of the action of the death drive. This is an isolation whose only fate is the uncertain and obscure state we describe by names suggesting an "unknown" that produces anxiety. The other clinical experience I mentioned—alienation in external reality—might, despite its possibly extreme seriousness, be a form of handling the most destructive terrors. I would venture to say that the repetitive behaviors in the transference (and in relation to others in the patient's life), occurring in this alienation in reality, represent attempts to deal with the primary trauma in a less catastrophic way. This trauma, driven by the death instinct in its most self-destructive form, gave rise to the primary split which, because it was not mitigated by an appropriate external object (good breast or good mother), caused the self to take up a position at a safe distance from the so-called bizarre objects (Bion 1957, 1958). Nevertheless these objects threaten the still undamaged parts of the self with an annihilating return.

REFERENCES

Bion, W. 1957. Differentiation of the psychotic from the non-psychotic personalities. In *Second Thoughts*, by W. Bion. London: Heinemann, 1967.

———. 1958. On hallucination. In *Second Thoughts*, by W. Bion. London: Heinemann, 1967.

Bott-Spillius, E. 1983. Some developments from the work of Melanie Klein. *Int. J. Psycho-Anal.* 64:321–32.

Folch, P., and Eskelinen de Folch, T. 1987. Negative transference: From split towards integration. *Bulletin of the European Psycho-Analytical Federation*, no. 28.

Freud, S. 1912. On the universal tendency to debasement in the sphere of love. *S.E.* 11:178–90.

———. 1920. *Beyond the pleasure principle. S.E.* 18: 3–64.

———. 1930. *Civilization and its discontents. S.E.* 21:59–145.

Joseph, B. 1983. On understanding and not understanding: some technical issues. *Int. J. Psycho-Anal.* 64:291–98.

Klein, M. 1946. Notes on some schizoid mechanisms. In *The writings of Melanie Klein*, Vol. 3. London: Hogarth, 1975.

Malcolm, R. Riesenberg. 1986. Interpretation: The past in the present. *Int. Rev. Psycho-Anal.* 13:433–43.

On Metapsychology
and Termination

ARNOLD M. COOPER

"Analysis Terminable and Interminable" is a work which several generations of psychoanalysts have found engrossing, puzzling, rich in ideas as well as disturbing because of its apparent pessimism. The paper was written after Freud had endured decades of suffering with cancer of the jaw and had undergone many operations. He had witnessed the rise of Nazism and was aware of the imminence of world war. He had also experienced the extraordinary success of psychoanalysis as a movement of thought in the Western world, and his ideas had triumphed over those of his detractors and competitors. Freud, however, never acknowledged this victory, maintaining that civilization, by its nature, could not be friendly to him and his ideas. In 1936, as he was being deluged with birthday congratulations and honors on his eightieth birthday, we wrote to Marie Bonaparte, "I am not easily deceived, and I know that the attitude of the world towards me and my work is really no friendlier than twenty years ago. Nor do I any longer wish for any change in it, no 'happy end' as in the cinema" (Jones 1957).

Freud, more than anyone else, had been responsible for the change that occurred after the early days of analytic triumph in the cure of the symptomatic neuroses, with dramatic results in short treatments. (Although today, as we review the early cases, the results were often less dramatic than they at first seemed.) In the later period there was an increasing demand on analysis to achieve more in the way of "deep" or "structural" change and a tendency for a dismissive attitude toward mere symptom relief as transference cure. Freud himself had always been wary about the possibility that analytic results emanated from suggestion rather than from specific interpretation, and that concern has not yet vanished from psychoanalysis. In trying to understand Freud's thinking in "Analysis Terminable and Interminable" it would be interesting to know how much analysis Freud himself was doing in the preceding few years, and what the duration of those analyses was; however, I have not been able to find this information.

Against this background it may be no surprise to find that this work is a restatement of some of Freud's most conservative points of view concerning psychoanalysis. It is a questioning of the status of psychoanalytic treatment and a daring foray into those aspects of psychoanalysis that some current workers consider the most advanced front of the field. As I shall try to illustrate, the conservatism lies in Freud's tenacity in retaining his metapsychology intact and in maintaining his focus on the neuroses rather than the character disorders, despite the advances of ego psychology that he initiated. His adventurousness lies in his opening the way to an understanding of the psychoanalytic process as an endless quest. But there is much more in the paper than these two concerns, and I shall also discuss some of the other thoughts that a reading of it generates.

This paper seems different, in both tone and intent, from some others written during the same period. "Constructions in Analysis" (1937), published in the same year, follows the more typical form of a Freud paper, beginning with a modest disclaimer of having anything new to say, followed by a bold and interesting idea—the understanding of delusions as an attempt at self-curative psychological construction based on an item of historical fact. This understanding was thus parallel to the analyst's use of history in creating constructions with a neurotic patient. *Moses and Monotheism* (1939), which Freud worked on only a little earlier, is, like a late Beethoven quartet, the work of an aged, sick, tormented master fearlessly pushing his genius beyond where anyone has ever trodden before. "Analysis Terminable and Interminable" is, in contrast, a presentation of the technical and theoretical problems confronting the analytic method at its present limits, a bit of summing up. Part of the fascination of the paper may derive from the slightly forbidding tone it takes toward analytic therapeutic enthusiasm. It is almost as if Freud is telling the numerous followers he has now accumulated to review their fervor for the method he has taught them and to ponder the limits of their capability. Freud is also, perhaps, informing these followers that he will not permit them easy profit and pleasure from his own hard-won findings, letting them know that they are not yet on solid ground and that much hard work and new information are needed. At its best psychoanalysis is not a comfortable profession. In fact, it is an "impossible" one.

Freud begins with a discussion of the social and financial desirability of shortening analysis, a goal even more to be desired today when analyses tend to be so lengthy. He discusses the practical aspects of ending analysis: "This happens when two conditions have been approximately fulfilled: first, that the patient shall no longer be suffering from his symptoms and shall have overcome his anxieties and his inhibitions; and secondly, that the analyst shall judge that so much repressed material has been made conscious, so much that was unintelligible has been explained, and so much internal resistance conquered, that there is no need to fear repetition of the pathological processes concerned" (p. 219). Freud then describes the theoretical meaning of the end of analysis, stating: "The analyst has had such a far-reaching influence on the patient that no further change could be expected to take place in him if his analysis were continued" (p. 219). He concludes that in the light of more modern demands for what analysis ought to be able to do, analysis surely will not get shorter (p. 224). These ambitious goals and this distinctive idea of the ideal termination form the backdrop for the remainder of the discussion.

Freud briefly refers to how analysis works, assuming that we know the basic answer to that problem and have little to add: "Instead of an enquiry into how a cure by analysis comes about (a matter which I think has been sufficiently elucidated) the question should be asked of what are the obstacles that stand in the way of such a cure" (p. 221). Freud seems to be closing the book on what analysis is and what its technical capacities are. He goes on, however, to raise questions about how we can tell when the process has been completed, and he reminds us that an analysis is not an event or a structure in itself, like a work of art, which may be examined in isolation from its context. It is rather a piece of a patient's life, and in that sense can never stand alone but can be examined only as a part of the patient's ongoing experience. He reviews the impediments to a "complete" analysis—for example, conflicts resistant to analysis because the original trauma was too great or because the instinct was too powerful, conflicts unanalyzable because they are not active during the span of the analysis, and insurmountable obstacles arising from derivatives of the death instinct. Finally, there are those hurdles that seem inherent in the elemental castration fear as it manifests itself differently in men and women. He questions how we can know that any successful analysis has produced a "permanent" cure, in the sense of "taming" an instinctual demand (p. 225) so that it will not again produce deformations of the ego in its defensive struggle with the instinct. He is explicit that his views on the analytic process have been influenced by his experience of doing training analyses and by treating severely ill patients in unending, although interrupted, treatment: "There was no question of shortening the treatment; the purpose was radically to exhaust the possibilities of illness in them and to bring about a deep-going alteration of their personality" (p. 224).

Early in the paper, Freud states the position that dominates the early part of his discussion and reveals the unusually conservative view of analytic work that I mentioned earlier. After defining health as a successful taming of instinct ("that is to say, the instinct is brought completely into the harmony of the ego, becomes accessible to all the influences of the other trends in the ego and no longer seeks to go its independent way to satisfaction" [p. 225]), Freud makes two interesting methodological decisions. First, he decides that, as between ego and instinct, the more important variable to be studied is the instinct. Second, he asserts that an understanding of instinct cannot be formed on clinical grounds but can be approached only through metapsychology. The decision to focus on instinct rather than on the ego and its interactions with the environment is crucial. Despite the great advances of ego psychology and the increasing interest in the superego, Freud returns to his earliest metapsychology, laying the greatest stress on the quantity of instinct and assuming that life can best be understood as the outcome of the struggle of the ego, the representative of civilization, against the instinct, which is always inimical toward the ego's aims. The constancy of this view in Freud's theory as well as in his personal philosophy is reflected in the quotation given earlier from the letter to Marie Bonaparte, in which he refuses to acknowledge the possibility of a friendly cultural attitude toward him and psychoanalysis. We should note that Heinz Hartmann (1937) was soon to publish his work on the preadaptedness of the instincts and on the conflict-free sphere of the ego. It seems likely that Freud knew of Hartmann's ideas, but this did not influence his work at all. He even seems to be cutting the ground from under Anna Freud and her advocacy of ego analysis and the analysis of defense as the core of analytic work. Although Freud is fully cognizant of this position, it interests him less than does a return to his earlier views of instinct. In effect, having described mental health as requiring a balance of id and ego strengths, he chooses to regard the ego's activities as a constant. He examines the consequences of changes in the force of an instinct and also those occasions in life when instinctual force increases, thereby rendering most defensive work impotent. It is almost as if Freud is putting a brake on ego psychology and on the direction it would take in the future toward emphasis on developmental vicissitudes.

This impression is reinforced by his second methodological decision, concerning the question of how instincts are tamed. Rather than pursue this as a clinical issue, perhaps by tracing the affective aspects of the transference, with affects seen as the mental representation of instincts, Freud decides that the only way to consider the question of taming the instincts is through the "witch," metapsychology. Quoting a famous line from Goethe, he says, "If we are asked by what methods and means this result [taming of the instinct] is achieved, it is not easy to find an answer. We can only say: 'So muss denn doch die Hexe dran!' ['We must call the Witch to our help after all!']—the Witch Metapsychology. Without metapsychological speculation and theorizing—I had almost said 'phantasying'—we shall not get another step forward. Unfortunately, here as elsewhere, what our Witch reveals is neither very clear nor very detailed" (p. 225). It is worth noting that despite whatever pessimism, or perhaps even depression, may color this paper, Freud never loses his wit, his pleasure in irony, his literary grace, and his total honesty with himself.

Our current attitudes toward the concept of instinct taming, one of the central ideas of Freud's early metapsychology, are vastly changed. The work of a generation of infant-observers and child psychoanalysts has cast serious doubt upon the validity of that idea. If we follow Freud in viewing the affects as the mental representatives of the instincts, Robert Emde (1984) and Daniel Stern (1985) in their work on affect development and on the development of the infant's tie to the mother have independently concluded that the concept of affect taming or instinct taming does not accurately represent what happens in development. The evidence indicates that the infant is at no point confronted with more instinctual charge or affect than he or she is biologically wired to handle. It must also be understood, however, that there is a profound change in point of view reflected in these current studies. The unit under study in the very young infant is the infant-mother pair, not the infant alone. There is increasing agreement among psychoanalysts that an interpersonal and object-relational point of view is essential when conceptualizing the baby's mental life; one cannot speak of the infant alone, since both biology and society dictate that the infant's affective (instinctual) life is regulated by the mother-infant dyad. In this view it becomes impossible to quantify instinct or affect, since whatever is constitutional always and immediately interacts with behaviors of the care-taker toward the expression of those tendencies. Furthermore, the behaviors of the mother favour the expression of certain aims and the suppression, perhaps even the deletion, of others. Contrary to Freud's strategy, the contemporary developmentalist is more likely to accept the infant's constitution (instinctual endowment) as relatively constant (although recognizing the importance of temperamental differences) and is consequently more likely to study the variable of mother-infant adaptation.

This brings us to Freud's second decision, to study instinct taming metapsychologically rather than clinically. It follows from what we have been describing that contemporary interest is likely to focus on the tension-regulating, soothing, and self-controlling capacities that begin to be internalized within the mother-infant dyad. Although guided by theory, the important studies of the workers we have mentioned, as well as those of Sandler (1987), Bowlby (1969), and Mahler et al. (1975), have all been efforts at clinical understanding. Under ordinary circumstances of child-rearing, the infant, enjoying the mediating and modulating effects of mothering, is in no greater danger from uncontrolled instinct or affect expression than is the older child or adult, who has largely, but never completely, internalized his regulating processes. The seemingly raw affective expressions of the infant are actually beautifully designed and quite effective for gaining appropriate mothering responses. Further, there is reason to consider that the bawling young infant does not yet have full-fledged psychological experiences, so that the question of the ego's being overwhelmed is not apposite. When he has a psychologically significant experience of frustration it seems likely that it is perceived as part of an interaction with a caretaker rather than as a totally internal event. Tension regulation, a developing task for the growing infant, is probably not quite the same as instinct regulation. However, tensions, which result from dysphoric affects, are reasonably subject to study. Instincts, as Freud correctly points out, can be considered only metapsychologically.

Turning to Freud's discussion of the requisite circumstances for the outbreak of psychic illness, it is likely that we would now make a different choice of the questions and methods for study. We would be interested in the changes in the environment and in object relations that could interfere with the ego's regulatory and control functions, and we would choose to study these circumstances clinically rather than metapsychologically. We would be concerned with how affects, object-relatedness, and self develop in organizational complexity and subtlety and with how the infant develops his or her own modulating and self-soothing capacities. Freud, in the language of his time, was also interested in these matters, as he makes abundantly clear in his exposition—when, for example, he compares the achievements in analysis with those of the normally developing ego. Why, then, should Freud have relinquished clinical observation in favor of metapsychological considerations? I do not know, but I will suggest two possible reasons. The first is that he lacked our current knowledge of infant development; the second, that he feared the loss of the distinctiveness of psychoanalytic psychology if the theory of instincts was significantly modified. This modification of the dual-instinct theory, if not an outright abandonment of it, has occurred in contemporary psychoanalysis—in my opinion, to the benefit of psychoanalytic theory and technique. Freud, and Anna Freud after him, were perhaps fearful of the "widening scope of psychoanalysis" and the resulting tendency toward broadening psychoanalytic conceptualizations. As I indicated earlier, it would be interesting to know if Freud was now also some distance from clinical psychoanalysis in his personal work, perhaps not having undertaken a new lengthy analysis for some years, and hence more drawn to theory.

We should also be aware that the challenge to the concept of instinct primacy was already developing during Freud's lifetime. Strachey's paper on analytic cure (1934) was written shortly before the paper we are discussing. In it he emphasizes the analyst's role as an object whose internalization helps in modifying the superego, the real agent of cure. I do not know whether Freud was aware of Strachey's paper. It is of interest that more recently Loewald (1960; Cooper 1986), eager to conserve Freud's metapsychology, including the concept of instinct, has nonetheless felt obliged to alter his own metapsychological ideas quite radically. He fully abandons the primordial antagonism of instinct and ego, adopting views much closer to those of Winnicott and others, and assumes that both instinct and ego develop out of a mother-infant matrix. One cannot even imagine the instincts apart from their developmental matrix. Here again, the concept of instinct taming gives way to a newer model of mutual adaptation, in which the object of study is the mental structure of object representations. One's aim can then be to assess the pliancy of the system and its accessibility to psychoanalytic alteration. We come closer here to clinical assessment than to metapsychological speculation. The antimetapsychology movement begun by George Klein may have gone too far in its effort to bring psychoanalysis back to its clinical roots, but we should surely welcome every opportunity to keep our discussion of a clinical issue such as termination of analysis on a clinical level. Freud was right in saying that the call upon metapsychology is a last resort, and, as we would now see it, he had not yet reached that last resort.

Throughout his discussion of clinical issues in this paper, Freud tends to assume that conflicts are relatively isolated from one another and that the ego has at its disposal specific repressive defenses directed toward each early instinctual conflict. He says, "The real achievement of analytic therapy would be the subsequent correction of the original process of repression, a correction which puts an end to the dominance of the quantitative factor" (p. 227). He goes on to express his doubt that this is ever realized, and thus the quantitative factor remains paramount. In a brilliant discussion of the treatment of neurosis Freud continues this line of thought, discussing the rigidity of the neurotic ego that results from its being locked in battle against an infantile danger: "The crux of the matter is that the defensive mechanisms directed against former danger recur in the treatment as *resistances* against recovery. It follows from this that the ego treats recovery itself as a new danger" (p. 238). Many contemporary analysts would add that the prospect of change is viewed as a danger by the neurotic ego not only because it threatens to awaken forbidden impulses, but also because any change of ego function or attitude threatens the sense of safety and coherence represented by the habitual and familiar. As Freud himself points out, "The adult's ego . . . finds itself compelled to seek out those situations in reality which can serve as an approximate substitute for the original danger, *so as to be able to justify, in relation to them, its maintaining its habitual modes of reaction*" (p. 238; italics added). One might interpret this as suggesting that the ego is more concerned with its own coherence and consistency than with the original danger. A key question for adult pathology is the degree to which the current problem is the continuing need to avoid an original danger, or is the process of miscarried repair itself, rigidified and internally perceived as the essential self. Today there is no agreement on this issue.

All this brings us to the interesting question Freud raises about the ability of analysis to insure the patient against future neurotic illness resulting from the revival of a conflict that is dormant at the time of the analysis. He concludes that such an insurance is not likely, since in analysis we cannot artificially revive a dormant conflict that causes the patient no anxiety at the time. Nor can we strengthen the ego against such a conflict, since it is inactive, and therefore the defenses involved do not appear in the analytic process. Many analysts today see the psyche as a fully interconnected web —enter at any point and, in principle, one has access to every other point. But Freud, the discoverer of so many different strands of psychic life, tended to think of them as more separated. One could, adopting the view of widespread internal connection, assume that an ego with a new degree of internal coherence and flexibility could handle the activation of a conflict even without analysis of that specific, previously dormant, conflictual matter. I will return to this interesting question at the end of this discussion, when I examine the narrative view of psychoanalysis in relation to termination. At issue is the question of the primacy of psychic conflict as a determinant of neurosis, as opposed to the prominence given to the weakness or abnormality of the structure of the self or ego. Again, although analysts have generally veered from the rather strict isolation of conflicts that Freud implies, there surely is no agreement today concerning how far we should venture from Freud's view. It is conspicuous that in this paper, unlike some earlier ones, Freud gives little attention to what we would now call the world of internal objects. In essence he avoids any aspect of mental representation except for the direct awakening of the original trauma. He also gives relatively little attention to the character disorders, which in modern psychoanalysis have rather fully replaced the neuroses as the object of our therapeutic intent. In fact, a number of the avenues of interest that had been opened up in *Inhibitions, Symptoms and Anxiety* (1926), particularly the opportunity to expand upon the role of affect in mental life and neurosis, are omitted.

Freud goes on to discuss some questions about psychic structure and gives a remarkably advanced view of the inheritance of personality characteristics, concluding that the fact that the ego has inherited (biological) characteristics removes the topographical distinction between ego and id. This leads him to a discussion of those special resistances that cannot be localized in a structure, which seem "to depend on fundamental conditions in the mental apparatus" (p. 241). He describes (1) adhesiveness of libido, (2) excessively mobile libido, and (3) excessive rigidity. I find this listing fascinating, because these three groups represent precisely those patients thought of today as suffering from forms of severe character disorder. These are of particular interest because of what we can learn from them about pre-Oedipal development and because of the potential responsiveness of some of these patients to pharmacologic agents.

The patients with "sticky libido" (group 1) could be described as those with excessive separation anxiety, often in borderline personality structures. Some would be regarded as having forms of panic anxiety with potential phobia formation. We would probably agree that there are important genetic elements in such characters, but we would look to pre-Oedipal development for an understanding of the clinging, unadventurous nature of these patients. Many of them prove to be responsive to a variety of antidepressant and anxiolytic pharmacologic agents. The patients in group 2 would probably be considered under the rubric of narcissism, analyzed in terms of a defective structure of the self that either fears attachment or has an incapacity for affective linkage. Again, we would now be interested in the nature of the object-relatedness that had developed in the earliest years and its revival in the transference. The third group is perhaps the most puzzling. One may raise questions about the plasticity of their neuronal structures as well as about their psyches. They are likely to be viewed as having suffered excessive pre-Oedipal damage from failure to establish empathic ties to caretaking persons. While we might share Freud's therapeutic pessimism, we would try to explore the narcissistic wounds that this rigidity may defend against. It is also perfectly clear that we are little, if at all, wiser today than Freud was in understanding this premature hardening of the psychodynamic arteries.

In continuing his exploration of the elements that make for therapeutic success or failure Freud discusses those characteristics of the analyst that make him effective. He expects "a considerable degree of mental normality and correctness," so that his defects will not interfere with his assessment of and response to the patient. He also "must possess some kind of superiority, so that in certain analytic situations he can act as a model for his patient and in others as a teacher" (p. 248). Finally, the analyst must have a love of truth. These attributes are interesting in the light of the current joke that some of the analysts of Freud's generation were so "crazy" that they would not be accepted for analytic training today. Despite his devotion to his concept of "psychic reality," Freud unabashedly maintains that the analyst's view of reality is superior to that of his patient and that it is necessary for the analyst to be someone who can be idealized. He clearly means that the analyst should have traits that *deserve* to be idealized; he is not referring simply to the patient's transference tendency to idealize. Freud lists these personal characteristics with no attempt to relate them to the theory of analytic therapy he has been discussing. But a very different theory of analytic change is implied in the idea of the patient modeling himself on a superior person, or internalizing a good object, than is implied in the idea of undoing repressions via interpretation. These two halves of the theory of cure are not discussed by Freud in this paper, although he often alluded to them elsewhere. The interpersonal context of the treatment process cannot be expressed easily in the language of intrapsychic conflict—a problem that persists in analytic theory.

It is curious that Freud, while acknowledging the increasing complexity, depth, and time that analysis takes, recommends for the analyst in training only a "short and incomplete" analysis for "practical reasons" that are not stated. Its purpose is simply to give a "firm conviction of the existence of the unconscious." Freud counts on the "processes of remodelling the ego" continuing spontaneously in the course of the young analyst's education and experience. Why should a short analysis continue spontaneously and satisfactorily for analysts and not for other creatures? Presumably this is because analysts are constantly immersed in psychodynamic processes and, once convinced of the unconscious, will continue to change themselves. One might infer that their model for the superior person of the analyst is Freud himself, and he takes it for granted that anyone committed to psychoanalysis will in a sense unconsciously continue to be his analysand.

At the same time Freud refers to the constant churning up of instinctual demands in the course of doing analytic work as a source of danger. As a result he suggests that "Every analyst should periodically—at intervals of five years or so—submit himself to analysis once more, without feeling ashamed of taking this step. This would mean, then, that not only the therapeutic analysis of patients but his own analysis would change from a terminable into an interminable task" (p. 249). It is safe to say that present-day psychoanalysts do not follow Freud's recommendation. Despite the frequency of second analyses, they are usually undertaken out of dissatisfaction with the training analysis (Cooper, ed., 1986), or because of a life crisis, and not because of a sense of accumulating instinctual pressure and the weakening of defenses. Should we interpret this as a failure of the seriousness of modern psychoanalysts, or as an indication that Freud was incorrect in suggesting that analytic work increased the instinctual danger to the practitioner? I suggest the latter hypothesis. If we abandon the instinctual perspective, we might consider that being a psychoanalyst is good for one's mental health. The opportunity to review the myriad defense mechanisms displayed by our patients and the almost automatic (and perhaps inevitable) comparison of one's own intrapsychic activity with what one has viewed in a patient provide innumerable occasions to bring preconscious thoughts and feelings into consciousness. Sometimes even previously unconscious conflicts may be brought to consciousness.

I believe that the analyst's position of helping others provides a relatively guilt-free opportunity for acknowledging one's own difficulties, with the disclaimer "the patient is worse off than I." While all sorts of instinctual arousals do occur in the course of conducting psychoanalysis, they are carefully bounded by the analytic situation, for the most part posing little threat of action, and their detection is condoned, even rewarded, by the code that demands constant self-scrutiny for precisely these currents within ourselves. Our ethic assumes that we bear in ourselves all the flaws of our patients, in different mixtures and quantities. We are also aware that the psychoanalyst in his professional role is not quite the same person as elsewhere in his life. In our protected role as psychoanalysts we are generally able to be far more selfless and empathic than in other life situations, in which we may perceive the threats to our feelings of safety far more keenly. It was a part of Freud's genius to design the psychoanalytic situation so that the psychoanalyst is skillfully protected from psychic risk.

In the last section of the paper Freud returns to one of his recurrent themes, the consequences of the anatomical distinction between the sexes. Here he finds a piece of the bedrock of psychoanalytic possibilities. In one of those statements that aroused feminine ire a few years ago he refers to the "repudiation of femininity," as it appears in both sexes, as a "remarkable feature in the psychical life of human beings" (p. 250). He rejects Ferenczi's claim of having successfully analyzed female penis envy and the male fear of passivity toward another male. He says:

> At no other point in one's analytic work does one suffer more from an oppressive feeling that all one's repeated efforts have been in vain, and from a suspicion that one has been 'preaching to the winds', than when one is trying to persuade a woman to abandon her wish for a penis on the ground of its being unrealizable or when one is seeking to convince a man that a passive attitude to men does not always signify castration and that it is indispensable in many relationships in life. The

rebellious overcompensation of the male produces one of the strongest transference-resistances. He refuses to subject himself to a father-substitute, or to feel indebted to him for anything, and consequently he refuses to accept his recovery from the doctor. No analogous transference can arise from the female's wish for a penis, but it is the source of outbreaks of severe depression in her, owing to an internal conviction that the analysis will be of no use and that nothing can be done to help her. And we can only agree that she is right, when we learn that her strongest motive in coming for treatment was the hope that, after all, she might still obtain a male organ, the lack of which was so painful to her.

But we also learn from this that it is not important in what form the resistance appears, whether as a transference or not. The decisive thing remains that the resistance prevents any change from taking place—that everything stays as it was. We often have the impression that with the wish for a penis and the masculine protest we have penetrated through all the psychological strata and have reached bedrock, and that thus our activities are at an end. This is probably true, since, for the psychical field, the biological field does in fact play the part of the underlying bedrock. The repudiation of femininity can be nothing else than a biological fact, a part of the great riddle of sex. It would be hard to say whether and when we have succeeded in mastering this factor in an analytic treatment. We can only console ourselves with the certainty that we have given the person analysed every possible encouragement to re-examine and alter his attitude to it. (Pp. 252–53)

With these remarks, Freud ends his paper, and his conclusion is a curious one, for it calls upon biology to explain a clinical difficulty, rather than sticking to analytic tools to try to understand, on purely psychoanalytic grounds, why castration anxiety is so intractable. This parallels an earlier strategy in this paper, reverting to metapsychology to understand how instincts are tamed. Possibly Freud was loath to return to the pre-Oedipal themes that he almost reluctantly uncovered in his paper "Female Sexuality" (1931). In an earlier paper (Cooper 1986b) I have suggested that castration anxiety attains its central role in mental life as the representative closest to consciousness of deeper, pre-Oedipal anxieties related to the loss of identity, or boundary, or body—to some form of annihilation fear related to earliest states of the forming self. Freud's reluctance to see the bedrock of psychic development as prior to the Oedipal phase seems particularly relevant in understanding his conclusions. It is almost as if he set the boundaries to psychoanalysis by claiming that whatever was beyond castration anxiety was pure biology.

We should note several points. Few analysts today would agree the "strongest motive in coming to treatment" of their female patients is "the hope that, after all, she might still obtain a male organ." Rather, without challenging the existence of penis envy, we believe that a significant portion of penis envy relates not to anatomy but to two aspects of penis symbolization —the penis as representative of male privilege, and the penis as a representation of successful separation from the powerful mother of the pre-Oedipal period. There are also important problems of self-esteem and object-relations that are not reducible to penis envy in any form. Freud gave no attention to the social attitudes toward femininity. His lack of interest in these concerns may relate to a hesitation to perturb or interfere with the assumption of unquestioned male authority. This may have impeded his capacity to analyze penis envy to a deeper layer.

The fascinating question of the masculine protest—the inability of a man to accept a passive attitude toward another man—is still quite unresolved. There is an implied demand on Freud's part for submission to him by his male patients—in fact, by all his patients. Treatment requires the patient's acceptance of subjection to the father, or at least the idea that he "receives" his recovery from the doctor. Freud seems to treat this as a fact rather than as a fantasy to be analyzed. He seems to believe that resistance to the passivity involved in the treatment situation refers to actual passivity in a real relationship with another person, the analyst, rather than to a frightening fantasy of passivity that is aroused in some males. There is a fine but important line between accepting one's recovery from the doctor and accepting with gratitude the doctor's role as *facilitator* of a recovery for which one is responsible. Today, many analysts would understand certain key aspects of passivity as being readily traceable to conflicts with the mother. In this view fear of passivity toward another male would represent a displacement of an earlier fear of a powerful mother. Alternatively, we observe homosexuals who are eager to be passive with another man while unconsciously enacting fantasies of being at the mercy of an all-powerful mother. Freud may have been right in his view of the bedrock, but it is worth querying his conclusion that the masculine protest and penis envy are basic fears rather than reflections of other underlying wishes and fears that may be analyzed. It would be preferable not to be in the theoretically uncomfortable position of having to assume that nature constructed a masculine world in which all females are doomed to special discomfort because of a biological antagonism to being feminine.

The idea of analytic bedrock (or "interminability") poses the question of what in the individual personality is inaccessible to analytic exploration although it does affect the analytic process. Freud's idea of the repetition compulsion would fit this description, as it is seen as a force in mental life, perhaps derived from the death instinct, not amenable to verbal exploration. This is implicit in his idea that "the presence of a power in mental life which we call the instinct of aggression or of destruction according to its aims, and which we trace back to the original death instinct of living matter," a power which is resistant to health or change, accounts for masochism and the negative therapeutic reaction (p. 243). A similar idea from a different point of view was put forth by Winnicott (1960) when he wrote of the normal adult as an "isolate" protecting himself from any intrusion into his true self. Some analysts have long held the view that our patients do not thank us for truly successful analyses that violate the innermost sense of the self. Many of our better analyzed cases remember very little of the analytic process and establish new and firm boundaries against outside intrusions of such depth. Assuming that there is a certain health involved in the protection of the inner self from intrusion, the more ambitious the analysis becomes, not only will it become more difficult, but it may also begin to cross into relatively nonpsychological areas of early pre-Oedipal patterning that are analyzable, at least initially, only by their nonverbal manifestations, rather than as free associations. These problems seem much more like a bedrock of analysis than the clinical obstacles described by Freud.

Apart from the particular arguments that Freud put forth in various parts of his paper, we should bear in mind what his overall clinical conclusions are and whether they ring true to our own analytic experience. Freud reminds us that we have no clear endpoints for termination in cases of character neurosis. We would have to agree. He reminds us too of the immanent nature of resistance to change in psychoanalysis. Whether or not they believe in a death instinct, most analysts are struck by the sluggish pace of analytic change, the seemingly endless repetition required during the analysis of transference and resistance, and the ubiquity of masochistic phenomena. Freud is surely right in his attitude of skepticism toward dramatic analytic success (p. 229). He emphasizes how small a role is played by knowledge itself and how the importance of the patient's depth of conviction concerning what he has learned about himself in analysis is critical. In fact, depth of conviction concerning the nature of the unconscious is considered by Freud to be the most important achievement of the training analysis. Again, we recognize the old problem of "knowing" versus "knowing" in analysis. Indeed, one could go on with a long list of Freud's extraordinary insights in this paper.

Finally, I want to discuss one of the ideas implicit in this essay that reaches to the very edge of modern literary and philosophical views of how we construct our universe. An important contemporary view of the psychoanalytic process brings to analysis ideas that originated in literary criticism, although they are foreshadowed in Freud's paper. Psychoanalysis, according to the hermeneutic view, is a process of narrative construction. Analyst and patient work together to create, during the course of the analysis, increasingly complex, coherent, and complete versions of the patient's life story. Beyond its most primitive core, the self consists of the history or narrative that links together the infinity of thoughts, feelings, and actions that constitute the person. In "Analysis Terminable and Interminable" Freud anticipates the most modern trend in contemporary literary criticism in suggesting that the person or life story or narrative never comes to genuine closure; there is no ending. Frank Kermode, a literary critic, suggests in *The Art of Telling* (1972) that there is no closure or genuine ending (termination, if you wish) to any great novel. This lack of ending is explicit in the modern novel, but novels have always been designed to provide for the continuing life of the characters and for continuing narrative interpretation. That is why any good novel is pertinent to any age and generates endless new exegesis of its text. Analysis, as Freud describes it in this paper, as well as literary criticism, generates endless endings; another version or interpretation of the story is always possible, and every rereading will generate additional meanings.

Kermode points out that the idea of a clear ending to a story is relatively new and was unknown in medieval literature, in which several different versions of a story existed side by side, with significant alterations of the tale and with no sense of contradiction nor any ending to the story. The modern narrative view of psychoanalysis, with its emphasis on large constructions rather than narrow interpretation of conflict, assumes that there are always multiple possibilities. Like a great novel, any human personality will appear different and will be differently understood under different conditions. For the novel, the different circumstance is the different culture that brings forth a reader who has a different understanding. For analysis the different circumstance is a new set of transference-countertransference relationships, and this difference can be regarded as occurring anew in each session or (more grossly) at different periods of a patient's life or with different analysts.

From this point of view the question that Freud raises of reawakening dormant conflicts takes on a different perspective. As indicated earlier, contemporary analysts are less likely to view conflicts as sequestered, each one having its own set of special defenses devoted to it. Taking a narrative point of view, we are likely to view the personality as intertwined, a complex skein in which all the knots are linked. Unraveling may proceed from any point and will lead toward all other points. Conflicts are not isolated but are ongoing aspects of the total personality, and the working through of some conflicts of significance will begin to have effects on others not apparent on the surface. It is a common experience, when doing analysis, that symptoms that have not been addressed during the analytic work disappear as a result of the reorganization of aspects of the character that were germane to other issues. Frequently, for example, mild phobias, sexual symptoms, and eating disorders "self-cure" in the course of an analysis that may be addressing narcissistic problems. Freud speaks as if the repertoire of conflicts is already encapsulated within the individual, to be uncovered by analysis. Many contemporary analysts are inclined to think that conflicts are unending, creative human acts, and that the overall level of personality organization will determine whether or not any one has pathological consequences. The issue of interminable analysis is not one of reawakening dormant conflicts but a realization that different perspectives on the person will *always* arise in the course of adaptation to new life situations. The adaptation of the personality in such different situations will bring different conflicts to the fore, and some of them will not have been predictable.

Having discussed many different points of view I wish to emphasize that we end in agreement with Freud. The "therapeutic" analysis is not one that has analyzed all dormant conflicts but one that has enabled a sufficient reorganization of ego capacities to take place so that there is a greater coherence of conscious and unconscious elements. There is an acceptance of unconscious trends into consciousness so that new aspects of unconscious conflicts and wishes can be available to an ego that is neither rigidly hostile to the unconscious trend nor passively intimidated before the evidence of an unacceptable wish. Beyond all the technical problems posed by Freud, this is his basic position. Analysis is indeed interminable as the human personality is constantly recreating itself. Our job as analysts is to try to push beyond the bedrock that Freud encountered, to increase this human possibility.

REFERENCES

Bowlby, J. 1969. *Attachment and loss*. Vol. I, *Attachment*. New York: Basic Books.

Cooper, A. M. 1986a. On "On the therapeutic action of psychoanalysis" by Hans Loewald: A psychoanalytic classic revisited. Paper presented to the Association for Psychoanalytic Medicine, New York.

———. 1986b. What men fear: The façade of castration anxiety. In *Psychology of men: New psychoanalytic perspectives*. New York: Basic Books.

Cooper, A. M., ed. 1986. *The termination of the training analysis: Process, expectations, achievements*. IPA Monograph, no.5.

Emde, R., and Harmon, R. J., eds. 1984. *Continuities and discontinuities in development*. New York and London: Plenum Press.

Freud, S. 1926. *Inhibitions, symptoms and anxiety*. S.E. 20:77–178.

———. 1931. Female sexuality. *S.E.* 21:223–46.

———. 1937. Constructions in analysis. *S.E.* 23:255–70.

———. 1939. *Moses and monotheism*. S.E. 23:3–138.

Hartmann, H. 1939. *Ego psychology and the problem of adaptation*. New York: International Universities Press, 1958.

Jones, E. 1957. *The life and work of Sigmund Freud*. Vol. 3. New York: Basic Books.

Kermode, F. 1972. *The art of telling*. Cambridge, Mass.: Harvard University Press.

Loewald, H. 1960. On the therapeutic action of psycho-analysis. *Int. J. Psycho-Anal.* 41:16–33.

Mahler, M. S.; Pine, F.; and Bergman, A. 1975. *The psychological birth of the human infant*. New York: Basic Books.

Sandler, J. 1987. *From safety to superego*. New York: Guilford Press; London: Karnac.

Stern, D. N. 1985. *The interpersonal world of the infant*. New York: Basic Books.

Strachey, J. 1934. The nature of the therapeutic action of psycho-analysis. *Int. J. Psycho-Anal.* 15:127–59.

Winnicott, D. W. 1960. Ego distortion in terms of true and false self. In *The maturational processes and the facilitating environment*, 140–52. New York: International Universities Press.

Instinct in the
Late Works of Freud*

ANDRÉ GREEN

"Analysis Terminable and Interminable" may be regarded as one panel of a triptych which, taken as a whole, forms Freud's testament. Whereas *An Outline of Psycho-Analysis* (1940; unfinished) brings together the essential points of psychoanalytic theory, *Moses and Monotheism* (1939) illustrates a nontherapeutic application of psychoanalysis. Freud here connects the cultural development of our Judæo-Christian civilization with the consequences of carrying out the murder of the father. This was a particularly significant factor for him, as the Oedipus complex, described as the nuclear complex of the neuroses, is also called the father complex. To give coherence to this group of works, the following subtitle for "Analysis Terminable and Interminable" could be imagined thus: "Why the Oedipus Complex Cannot Be

*It is impossible to avoid mentioning some of the problems of translation regarding Freud's term *Trieb*. Dr. Green's original article in French uses the word *pulsion*. The English translation from the French has the choice between *drive* or *instinct*. We know that American authors most frequently prefer the first and that English authors generally use the second. Dr. Green has accepted the suggestion to follow the English usage. It does not follow from this adoption that the gap between Freud's concept *Trieb* and the biological concept *instinct* is narrowed in Dr. Green's thought.

Disposed Of." The reason is easily misunderstood: instead of blaming this failure on what precedes it and is both prior and external to it, we should hold responsible that which prefigures it too early or too suddenly. Its primitive forms are expressed through instincts, and it may be assumed without distorting Freud's ideas that, however elementary their manifestations, they are nevertheless the vectors of an instinctual vocation which the Oedipus complex performs fully but does not create alone and, so to speak, by itself.

"Analysis Terminable and Interminable" is uniquely valuable for giving us a quite precise impression of Freud's conception of psychoanalysis as a therapeutic method. Here Freud inevitably resorts to concepts in order to take account of clinical experience. At first, he tries to use only those which seem to him essential for an understanding of the factors involved in the genesis of the neuroses and of the way in which they are revealed by psychoanalytic treatment, principally as obstacles to the achievement of the goals of analysis, "the freeing of someone from his neurotic symptoms, inhibitions and abnormalities of character" (p. 216). The achievement of this objective would be an ideal result, because Freud, throughout his paper, stresses the relevant limitations, not all of which are to be blamed on the analyst's incompetence.

The more Freud develops his ideas, the more the initial concepts, whose field is restricted, are seen to assume a wider speculative range—especially for the purpose of explaining the failures of analysis. This causes many of his colleagues to disagree with him and to put his opinions down to his pessimism, aggravated by old age. In fact, Freud himself had for many years ceased to regard himself as "a therapeutic enthusiast," if indeed he had ever been one. Is this speculation justified? For a long time, its critics concentrated on the hypothesis of the death instinct, an inherently controversial subject. As it happens, the development of psychoanalytic thought was to show that it is the concept of instinct itself, understood in the most general sense possible, that has given rise to significant reservations. I shall therefore devote this paper to instinct in general and disregard the thorny question of the death instinct.[1] I shall begin by briefly reviewing some present-day viewpoints and shall then consider whether the replace-

---

1. Interested readers may refer to *La Pulsion de mort* (The death instinct), published in French by Presses Universitaires de France in 1986, a record of a European Psycho-Analytical Federation Symposium at which I expressed my opinion on the subject.

ments proposed by these criticisms do in fact cover the same field as Freud's theory.

As we know, recent reformulations of psychoanalytic theory are aimed at the Freudian theory of instincts, or drives. Many authors criticize Freud's ideas in this respect because they consider Freud's postulation of a biological foundation to mental life to be questionable, either because, in their view, mental life implies a discontinuity with the biological organization, or because it is impossible to find a link between the findings of modern biology and the content of the instinct concept. In other words, such a gulf has opened up between the biology of Freud's time and that of today that the hypotheses of psychoanalysis seem even more improbable to the biologists, while the knowledge we owe to the biologists seems more and more inadequate to explain the phenomena which are the subject of psychoanalysis. I do not confine this observation to the contemporary controversy involving the "instinct" of the biologists and ethologists on the one hand and the Freudian "instinct" [*Trieb*] on the other, but wish to extend it to the overall conceptions thought to be at the root of mental life which underlie the ideas of the neurobiologists and those postulated by Freud.

The psychoanalysts, for their part, have tended to interpret Freud's ideas restrictively. Hence, as neurotic structures gradually gave way on the couch to nonneurotic ones, an entire foundation of rationality that had underlain psychoanalytic thought began to break up. After all, if neurosis is "the negative of perversion" and if perversion is the more or less direct expression of instinctual functioning, then it seems that we should conclude that replacement of the clinical criterion of "neurosis" by another criterion, such as "nonneurosis," could have the consequence of revealing a parameter other than that of instinct. In fact, with the passing of the years, it may be wondered whether the analytic community as a whole has not been more reluctant than it has wanted to appear to be to admit the existence of instincts other than the strictly sexual and aggressive ones and whether, for example, the idea of "ego instincts" has ever been truly assimilated by psychoanalysts. This means that, at bottom, psychoanalysts were gradually returning to a prepsychoanalytic conception of instinct and also of the ego, but have managed not to go back to the pre-Freudian era by preserving other, less problematic psychoanalytic concepts (for instance, the mechanisms of defense against anxiety).

Below I shall briefly outline some of the different viewpoints that have been proposed. I shall not go into detail, as my intention here is merely to recall the current alternatives.

Those Who Radically Reject the Concept of Instinct. In the field of Freudian psychoanalysis (in the broad sense), this group includes primarily Fairbairn, for whom the concept of object relations replaces that of instinct, and Guntrip, who extended Fairbairn's theory. More recently, some American authors have tried to split Freud's work in two, distinguishing his metapsychological views, which they consider not to have stood the test of time, from his clinical conceptions, which they wish to reformulate by a new theory dispensing with the concept of instinct. They consider that psychoanalysis is concerned with phenomena connected with motivation and meaning and that these phenomena would be better understood with either the adoption of more manifestly psychological concepts (M. Gill) or a more explicit reference to language, on which analytic experience is based. This change may be expressed in a specific approach (such as the "action language" of R. Schafer) or included in a wider whole of the hermeneutic type (M. Edelson).

Those Who Relativize the Concept of Instinct. Melanie Klein continued to adhere to Freud's instinctual dualism, although she interpreted it very differently. She also defended the idea of an object relation from the beginning of life. On this point, she differed both from Freud and from Fairbairn, who eliminated the fundamental role of instinct from his theory. However, as the ideas of the Kleinian school developed, the balance maintained by Klein between the expression of instincts and object relations was to shift increasingly in favor of object relations, archaic anxieties, and primitive defenses.

While acknowledging the importance of instinctual life, Winnicott postponed its beginnings until after the formation of a primitive ego capable of observing its effects, which, for him, were therefore manifested only secondarily. However, Winnicott is almost alone among contemporary theorists in proposing a theory of symbolization at the meeting point of the separation between inside and outside; he differs in this respect from Melanie Klein, who regards this merely as a process involving only the internal objects, and from Lacan, who associates it with its connection with language.

Ego psychology disputes the Freudian idea of a primitive id from which the ego is differentiated. It therefore postulates a separate origin for the two agencies and even maintains that a conflict-free area exists in the ego. This school was bound to place a restriction on the influence of the id. Again, in replacing the death instinct by the concept of aggression on a par with erotic libido, it tempered the radicalism of Freud's last theory of instincts. This is true even if Hartmann remained convinced of the importance of instincts, wrongly expecting that the future would acknowledge that their influence was greater than it was thought to be at the time. The relativization was to be further emphasized by Kohut, who postulated an opposition between instincts on the one hand and the self and the vicissitudes of narcissism on the other. He thus distanced himself from the Freudian thesis that narcissism originates from transformations of the ego *instincts*. These theoretical changes favor a countertransference attitude tending more toward empathy at the expense of analysis in the Freudian sense.

Finally there is Lacan, who, while acknowledging the central position of instinct in Freud's theoretical edifice, subordinated instinct to the primacy of the *signifier*. Although Lacan tried to give the *signifier* a psychoanalytic meaning different from that developed by Saussure for linguistics, the differences between the *signifier* of Lacan and that of Saussure were never sufficiently clarified.

Those Who Retain the Essentials of the Concept of Instinct but Introduce Changes in Detail. Included in this group are, among others, all the non-Lacanian French theorists. Since their reformulations of Freudian theory do not call its fundamentals substantially into question, I shall not consider them in detail here.[2]

This outline of the main schools represented in contemporary psychoanalytic theory does not claim to be a review of the literature but is simply an attempt to describe the general trends that have emerged in discussions among psychoanalysts. The development of psychoanalytic thought described is attributable just as much to clinical experience as to the wish to benefit from knowledge acquired outside psychoanalysis itself (some of it gathered by psychoanalysts working in related fields). The reasons for this are easily understood and can be summarized as follows:

---

2. Among many possible differences in the interpretation of the Freudian concept, Laplanche's deserves a special mention. Laplanche thinks that the concept of the *Trieb* is still useful, though he transforms its contents with the notion of the "source-object." The introjected object functions as a source of excitation just as in Freud's notion of the source of the instinct.

1. The genuine difficulty of understanding the complexity of the psychoanalytic material of nonneurotic structures other than by a paraphrase in psychoanalytic terminology.

2. The hope of finding help in fields where the facts are decoded by conceptual tools lacking the ambiguities, obscurities, and complexities of the theoretical instruments of Freudian thought.

3. The need to transmit readily assimilable knowledge.

4. The wish to reduce the difference between analytic thinking and the approaches of related disciplines, to help keep psychoanalysis within the academic and scientific community.

However, these circumstantial reasons cannot be allowed to prevail. In my view, the important point is not whether a postulate of psychoanalytic theory conforms or does not conform to reality, or is acceptable or unacceptable by the criteria of science, but whether the concept offered to me makes it possible *in its generality* for me to imagine mental functioning. The varying images of such functioning presented by individual clinical cases may be regarded as aspects that can be glimpsed by virtue of the concept.

Following this long parenthesis, let us now return to Freud's paper. We see that Freud remains as far as possible within a general register in relation to our problem. With regard to instinct, his statements are limited to the widest possible formulations, always expressed in pairs (adhesiveness–inertia of the libido, Eros–Thanatos, heterosexuality–homosexuality, masculinity–femininity). Freud does not here mention the different components of an instinct (source, pressure, object, aim), and it is impossible to say whether or not he has given up this formulation. But he seems to remain faithful to the idea of contrasting pairs.

The material submitted for analysis takes the form of a whole whose different components can be connected with either the ego or the instincts, conceived in terms of relative forces that limit each other. This pair of forces is supplemented by a random factor—random in regard to its determining potentiality—of trauma. According to its timing and form, trauma may appreciably modify the characteristics of one or the other or both of these two determinants, ego and instincts. This configuration sometimes gives rise to pathological organizations that Freud declares to be of their essence inaccessible to psychoanalytic therapy, and sometimes to pathologies which turn out to be inaccessible only after the treatment has gotten under way.

Hence there is a margin of unforeseeability at the beginning, leading sometimes to success and sometimes to failure. All Freud's interest is focused on
the latter case.

However, when Freud is induced to take account of historical situations
going far back toward the beginning of life, he is compelled to point out that
the distinction between the ego and the id (that is, the instincts) ceases to be
of interest from a speculative point of view. However, it seems to me that it
remains interesting from a theoretical and clinical viewpoint, because what
is implied here is that the precariousness of the organization of the ego
makes that ego vulnerable to the demands of the instincts. Consequently, the
effect of early trauma is liable to be confused with that of an unexpected
strengthening of instinct. Alternatively, the trauma, if very early, could give
rise to a topographic upheaval, as if the weight of the instinctual burden
were applied from the outside. This would make it necessary to adopt measures of mental closure and restriction that would singularly limit the ego's
ability to grow by the assimilation of later sources of pleasure.

Of what does trauma consist? Although Freud's text constantly alludes to
this question, it does not really answer it. If it is taken for granted that
trauma affects the ego's fragile capacities for organization, this does not
mean that Freud is maintaining that trauma always represents a victory for
the instincts insofar as they thus escape from the influence of the ego. We
must beware of confusing victory of the instincts with satisfaction of the
libidinal instincts alone. The hypothesis of two major groups of antagonistic
instincts obviates this possible confusion, as the consequence of preventing
the satisfaction of erotic instincts may be the deployment and satisfaction of
destructive instincts. Victory of the instincts and failure of the ego will
therefore ultimately mean the impossibility of satisfying instincts through
an object that not only imposes cultural prohibitions (the negative aspect)
but also displays the wide variety of forms of satisfaction offered by its
existence (the positive aspect).[3]

Freud thus seems to want to insist on the rightful autonomy of instinctual
life, namely, the fact that it is not reducible—to acquired experience. Experience can and should modify the expression of instinctual life, but it does
not affect the principles that lie at the root of its functioning. Freud reminds
us that it is connected with biological life at the time of crises governed by a

---

3. This paper takes no account of the modifications that have been made to the
theory of trauma, such as the hypothesis of cumulative trauma.

determinism associated with the structure of the human organism—even if in such cases the psychic events linked with the physiological upheavals caused by the crises take part in the creation of symptoms.

It is justifiable to conclude that Freud postulates in this paper, more clearly than ever before, the existence of a structural triad made up of the following elements:

1. *An internal element* which is the basic datum point: *the instincts*. These have fundamental demands, which will be modified by experience in such a way that their satisfaction is compatible with demands of another type—that is, cultural demands—with a certain latitude allowing a flexible response to individual circumstances. This means that parts (but only parts) of the instincts will allow themselves to be transformed by joining together with other, historically later structures. On the other hand, those parts that have not undergone transformation but are only repressed may reappear in all their original strength, owing either to the failure of later formations or to "endogenous" overactivation. This last may in turn outstrip the retaining capacities of the agencies which forbid their expression in the more or less primitive state.

2. *An external element*, which acts in two ways through *the object*. It may act positively, in which case the object assists the constitution of the ego in its attempt to master the instincts. This function is performed by a process of sorting, the aim of which is to refuse expression to instincts judged to be incompatible with the maintenance of a relation with the object *and* to tolerate those that remain compatible with and even necessary for development, by making them accessible to other influences. Or it may act negatively, through trauma, whose onset is variable and whose effects are not unequivocal. In some cases trauma gives rise to excessive, premature stimulation of instincts, disorganizing the nascent mastery of the ego and forcing the subject into a compulsion to repeat the premature stimulation. In other cases, the trauma may cause inhibitions that deprive the ego of its instinctual cathexes. This may also occur in the event of an internal intensification without the action of trauma. Character abnormalities may have a comparable etiology.

3. *A mediating element, the ego*, which is caught between contradictory demands:

   a. The demands of the unacceptable instinctual stimulations, which must be rejected.

b. The demands of instinctual satisfactions necessary for its own organization—that is, for the strength it acquires through the pleasures it incorporates. This strength is essential if the instincts are to become susceptible to the propositions of the object. It must also supply the mechanisms of defense with the energy they need to combat unacceptable instinctual demands and to transform the instincts that have to be accessible to other influences.

c. The demands of the object (in Freud's text, reality). Plainly, this last element is the one most liable to serious misappreciation, stubborn illusion, and blockages in the functioning of the ego corresponding to fixation in the field of instinct.

This conception is structural not only because its components are found in every human being but also because it defines the meaning of psychic activity, which is itself involved in the conflicts to which it necessarily gives rise. In these conflicts, either the internal or the external element may predominate according to circumstances, and in this regard we are bound to take account of the capacities of the mediating element, the ego, whose attributes are not determined entirely either by the first of the other factors, the second, or both in combination.

Freud's structural conception implies a postulate of paramount importance, *that of the heterogeneity revealed by analysis of the fundamental components of mental life, which appears phenomenologically to be unitary in spite of the discontinuity between consciousness and the unconscious.*

This structural conception is supplemented in Freud by two other parameters. The first is the quantitative factor, which may play a part at any time in the history of the individual. It may even at a late stage call into question the equilibrium achieved by the subject between the two poles of the internal and external elements described above. The second parameter, by contrast, increases the importance of early traumas and their action in the form of lasting and unmodifiable (as Freud no doubt saw them) alterations of the ego. However, it must be understood that whenever Freud mentions traumas, they always have the result of preventing the integration of instincts into the ego. This makes it impossible for the subject to withstand the pressure of the strength of the instinct, the source of the entire dynamics of the psyche, and makes the subject susceptible to influences of another type, the components of cultural life.

The ego's mastery of the instincts is relative and is responsive to the demands of human cultural life in general and to the demands of a particular social milieu.

The aim of all modern psychoanalytic research has been to throw more light on the part played by early influences in bringing about greater or lesser degrees of incapacity. However, it has gradually modified Freud's basic axioms. According to Freud, instincts are knowable to us only through their derivatives and can be apprehended only within a complex configuration that also includes their effects (defenses) and in which the ego, even in its most primitive form, is already involved. Moreover, the object seems to be relevant only as a function of trauma. Later workers have endeavored to broaden the frame of reference to encompass the whole field of relations between the ego of the young human being and his primary object, the mother, in the hope of clarifying Freud's intuitions and making them more useful for the purpose of theoretical conceptualization.

The broadening of the frame of reference has given rise to an increasingly psychological or personality-related approach.[4] For instance, separation-individuation is emphasized nowadays as an essential activity of the ego. This was certainly glimpsed by Freud in *Inhibitions, Symptoms and Anxiety* (1926), but he ultimately relates these processes to loss of the object capable of satisfying the instinct or mastering it psychically. He says, "The reason why the infant in arms wants to perceive the presence of its mother is only because it already knows by experience that she satisfies all its needs without delay. The situation, then, which it regards as 'danger' and against which it wants to be safe-guarded is that of non-satisfaction, of a *growing tension due to need*, against which it is helpless" (*S.E.* 20:137). Systematic, detailed study of these situations suggests that anxiety or the anticipation of danger seems to go far beyond instinctual life. However, at this point we find that the misunderstanding relates to our present-day conception of instincts as compared with Freud's use of the term.

Freud was well aware of the indeterminacy of the hypothesis of the instincts. We know that, before his time, the term *instinct* or *drive* [*Trieb*]

4. When Freud speaks of personality, he is referring to the "psychical personality," as it is manifested through the interplay of the three agencies. In my opinion, this is very different from the use that is made of the word when it is stated that psychoanalysis is a "science of the personality," which, by contrast, suggests a unifying and stabilizing reference where Freud principally sees division and instability, and constantly calls into question the appearance of unity.

was already in use in the general and specialized literature in German. Although lip service is paid to the oft-quoted statement that "the theory of the instincts is . . . our mythology," the impression remains that the reason it is mentioned is to try to get rid of this reference to the myth as quickly as possible because of its unfortunate overtones of mystery and even mystification. In the most favorable case, Freud's insistence on a biological foundation for the psyche will be put down to a survival or vestige of romantic naturalism. Freud therefore stands accused of an obsolete biologism. But biologism cannot be blotted out of the psychoanalytic literature by discarding its embarrassing propositions. On the contrary, a fictional "metabiology" is replaced by a realistic psychobiology which has the disadvantage, compared with Freud's ideas, of tending toward oversimplification.

Freud's fictional metabiology has always appealed to sexuality as a foundation for the theory of instincts. It is noteworthy that Freud seems to have found it necessary in all cases to contrast this fundamental nucleus of mental life with another, supposedly antagonistic group of instincts. This is a way of further intensifying the obstacles to the expression of sexuality—first, one has a factor of a different (psychological) kind with a different structure —the ego, and, second, one postulates a factor of the same kind that pursues an opposite objective. Mental life is constructed from materials with different properties (for example, the capacity for making demands or for repetitive insistence, the capacity for displacement or transference, the capacity for representability or representational transformation, the capacity for isolating selected features and for logically connecting relations, and the capacity for stagnation or renewal of cathexes). Freud tries to define these by reducing them to fundamental constituents bound up with the various agencies: what perception is to the ego, and the ideal function to the superego, instinct is to the id. He insists on these fundamental distinctions because each sphere possesses a potential for development that is proper to it and has specific ways of influencing the other spheres. Even if overlapping mechanisms can be observed (either in pathology or on a temporary basis), the reference to these intrinsic specificities appears to be the best guarantee for distinguishing the various fields that make up experience. Thus the reference to instinct, surely the most imprecise of the three—perhaps because it is the most primitive and hence the least differentiated—separates out within the mind that which cannot be connected either to reality or to the version of reality transformed by a desire for perfection (idealization). Logically, of course, the other two fields are defined in relation to the instinctual universe. Reality is defined as an external space that is the depository of the conditions of satisfaction of instincts (that is, fantasy is inevitably insufficient). The ideal is similarly a psychic condition in which the relinquishing of satisfaction can take place, either by obedience to an authority or by choice of a value judged to be more important than satisfaction.

It should therefore be clear that the reference to instinct cannot be eliminated, that it cannot be reduced to the commonly advanced idea of need, because it implies not only the correction of a lack but also a demand for pleasure. As Freud says, this is a bonus which assumes the same peremptory quality as a bodily need, although there is no biological justification for according it the benefit of this combination. In fact, by never losing an opportunity to point out that the *Trieb* expresses a bodily demand, Freud is reminding us that his distinction between animal instinct and human *Trieb* —the huge potential for substitution of aims and objects—has another side. Returning to the body means recalling the limits set to the transformation of instincts and also offering an explanation of the fixed, repetitive, and obstinate character of certain organizations that persist in spite of their anachronism and the suffering they cause. Perhaps this is because this suffering is not incompatible (for the unconscious) with forms of satisfaction that can, in this way, short-circuit any censorship that would prevent their expression on the level of the ego. However, it is important to note here that the bodily demand in question is an inseparable combination of a demand for satisfaction and a demand *for the object*, one capable of providing the satisfaction, after the failure of the detour of substitutions of object and aim or fixation on certain substitutive forms. It thereby probably establishes some highly unconsciously condensed conflictual and relational foci.

It seems to me that the confusion of contemporary thinking about instinct centers on this point. The semantics of the concept of instinct [*Trieb*] remain unanalyzed, and it is seen only as the humanized descendant of animal instinct. It is then easy to show that what is observed cannot be confined within the narrow field of the instinctual (whether animal or human) owing to the wealth of relational implications which can be inferred, even when the observation concerns something that would tend to be placed in this category of psychic phenomena. Although that which is to be accounted for usually lies *outside* the instinctual field or at least a long way away from its direct expression, this undeniable fact is not the point. What is lost in stopping there are the references to fundamental conceptual hypotheses that give the concept of instinct its operational value.

I deliberately use the word *operational* because, on a simple descriptive level, the hypothesis of instinct accounts better for the clinical facts than the alternative theses of object relations, meaning, adaptive function, and so on. All these alternatives leave hardly any place in their explanatory development for the impression that a part of psychic life has succeeded in seizing control of the direction of all of this life, either by dragging it along an undesired path or by paralyzing its course, against the wishes and interests of the individual concerned. The situation appears anachronistic, and change seems to carry within it a threat of disorganization. When we recall that instinct expresses a bodily demand, we are allusively specifying this as the possible location of an interface between a lack on the one hand and an object on the other. If we call this an object relation, we are emphasizing the fact that the bodily demand presupposes not only a "something" but also a "someone" with whom it waits to be connected. However, if this someone is introduced too early, thus weighting the scales in favor of the object, there is a danger of minimizing or underestimating the character of a psychic demand that suggests the comparison with need or animal instinct, although it differs from it profoundly. In this way, the *concept* of instinct relates to a reality that is unknown but can be described as a wandering force that searches without knowing exactly what it is searching for. It finds it almost without having searched for it, or gives the impression of having obscurely searched for something else, and *retroactively* discovers the meaning of its lack of satisfaction. The fundamental link between the instinct and satisfaction, which is presumed to put an end to the lack, is perhaps more appropriate for describing what does not suit this satisfaction than what conforms to its anticipation.

The other side of the coin of original instinctual indeterminacy is the function assigned by Freud to it in the opposition of Eros and destruction and, in another form, of heterosexual–homosexual and male–female relations. These ideas are too metaphysical for many present-day psychoanalysts who are concerned to abide by the restrictions on speculation that scientists impose on themselves. Yet these hypotheses appear only as generalizations derived from *observation of the most trivial facts of existence*. This is proved by the examples Freud uses as evidence in his paper. There is nothing that does not allude to the most common relations that link human beings together. Those who scorn these speculations take care not to advance others with equivalent or superior explanatory ability.

In assigning an ordering role in psychic life to the dual opposition of Eros–destruction and male–female, Freud was implicitly laying down axioms about the relations between nature and culture, relations in which man is involved profoundly by virtue of his dual biological and cultural heritage.

There is a significant change of tone in "Analysis Terminable and Interminable" between Freud's exposition, at the beginning, of the practical difficulties that he tries to make comprehensible by using essential concepts in a down-to-earth way and the speculative tendency of the closing sections. It is impossible not to suspect that this variation in discursive style may be due to Freud's having felt that his argument was insufficiently convincing. But it also reflects Freud's fear that his guiding hypotheses might gradually be lost sight of. The entire paper surely is full of anxiety about the shortening of analysis associated with Rank's schematization of neurotic nosogenesis. Another worry, less clearly expressed, might be directed, less closely, at Ferenczi, in that Freud felt that Ferenczi's final orientation attached too much importance to the object and hence to trauma. For this reason Freud gives the last word to the instincts, elevating them to a level on which they may even encounter the forces—attraction and repulsion—that govern the physical world.

Freud indeed seems to be neither able nor willing to listen to the voice of Ferenczi, which nevertheless obsessed him, as his paper continues the debate with Ferenczi after his death. Freud may have been so irritated by Ferenczi's criticisms concerning the attitude of the analyst that he rejected his disciple's technical innovations indiscriminately, along with his etiological views. Nowadays, however, the work of Ferenczi between 1928 and 1933 is at the root of the renewal of present-day psychoanalytic thought. This is not only evident in the developments of the Hungarian school, as is often pointed out, but also in, for example, Winnicott. Ferenczi's own contributions, of course, never involved any criticism of Freud's concept of instinct. He gave an even better demonstration than Freud himself of the effects of the meeting between instinct and object in his paper "Confusion of Tongues between Adults and the Child." This does not in my view call into question the truth of Freud's concept of instinct.

However, if we wish to narrow the gap between the "clinical" use of the concept of instinct and its "speculative" use (that is, even beyond metapsychology), taking account of the textual differences between the beginning and the end, then we should presumably refer to *An Outline of Psycho-Analysis*. Here, Freud provides some clarifications of his last theory of instincts that have not always been noticed, concerning the relations between

Eros and sexuality. Analysis of the text reveals three levels: (1) *Eros*, the name given to the fundamental instinctual group made up of the instincts of life or love; (2) *libido*, the indicator or representative of this instinctual group; and (3) the sexual *function* (no longer the sexual instinct), the field of psychic activity by which Eros can best be known.

This final formulation has, of course, important consequences, not only because it includes sexuality in a wider whole while according it the property of being a privileged means of access to knowledge of the entity Eros, which is knowable only through its manifestations, but also *because it implicitly combines sexuality and love at one and the same time*. This gives rise to an important semantic shift whereby, in our view, the object—through the explicit reference to a love instinct—is accorded a position of paramount importance compared with its situation in the earlier instinctual theories —namely, the theories of the sexual instinct.

The position assigned to sexuality in the biological heritage derives from its generational dimension—for the species and the individual. While it may be said that man, in the scale of living beings, is a denatured animal, that is, one capable of following pathways remote from those apparently prescribed by Nature for the animal species, human sexuality nevertheless retains its generational power—the ability to engender psychic structures. This is because its transformations necessarily entail an object. The relation to the object becomes an essential mediation for the dual engendering, by virtue of the complexity assumed by the working of the mechanisms of binding and unbinding of *intrapsychic* and *intersubjective* relations. The replacement of sexual instincts by love or life opens up a whole new field for consideration.

Thus, while Freud seems to have evolved toward a less strictly naturalistic but perhaps more final conception, this change has the heuristic advantage of conceiving of the Oedipus complex not only as a stage but also as a germination that includes the potentialities of its development through what we have called the instinctual vocation. Hence, contrary to appearances, the obstacles to the efficacy of analysis, whether due to instinct, the ego, or trauma, ultimately act convergently. They prevent infantile sexuality from reaching the culminating point of its development, which not only marks the end of a phase of life but, as it were, *constitutes the symbolic end of an entire life* by hindering the instincts, in their relations with objects, from evolving toward an acceptable Oedipus complex in cultural life. Infantile sexuality thereby becomes fixated to premature, precipitate, and over-condensed oedipal forms which are ultimately very difficult, if not impossible, to analyze because they cannot achieve full deployment of the instincts onto objects, thus highlighting the fundamental states of psychic activity, of Eros and destruction, masculinity and femininity. The emergence of these states is important not only because it reveals "evolution" in the child but because this evolution brings him into harmony with the *hidden* states of adult mental functioning.

It is perfectly clear to today's analysts that Freud underestimated the role of the object. Present-day clinical practice powerfully illustrates the vital part the object plays in psychoanalytic therapy, in intensification of transference – countertransference relations, and in reconstructions of the hypothetical past of our patients, as well as in what we have learned from studies of child-hood. In my view, however, if the instinctual factor is diluted within other references, we are liable to lose sight of the specificity Freud accorded to it.

This specificity is illustrated in the permanence of the tendency toward conflict, a tendency that exists within the instinctual entity itself—between the two major groups of instincts—and is reflected between instinctual life as a whole and the ego. It is subsequently taken over by the relations between the ego and the superego. The contradictory nature of instincts is expressed best in this sentence in the *Outline*: "Though they are the ultimate cause of all activity, they are of a conservative nature" (*S.E.* 23:148). They are there-fore necessarily involved in the broadening of mental life and its diversifica-tion due to their ability to change their aim and object, but at the same time they prove resistant to changes and developments that would be excessively at variance with their fundamental demands.

The work of psychoanalysis cannot be characterized either by adaptation or by maturation. From our point of view, it merges with the objective of the mental apparatus when confronted by instincts—which are an integral part of that apparatus. Just as the instincts "seek representation," psychoanalysis can have no other aim than the working out of the activity of representation in the widest possible sense. This is in fact where the entire difficulty resides, because psychoanalysis takes as its starting point the most sophisticated form of this representational activity—language—in an attempt to regain access to the forms that are most remote from it in structural and historical terms. By going back so far toward the origins, it retraces and uncovers the line of development of mental life from instinct to language.

The acknowledgment of such forces in everyone—including the psycho-analyst—totally contradicts our fond idea of mastery over our existence, choices, and destiny and opposes our wish for unlimited perfectibility. Similarly, it is also conceivable that the role of the object, underestimated by Freud, be stressed in the structuring of mental functioning. But this involves a danger of the replacement, in successive shifts, of psychoanalysis by a psychoanalytic psychology, as an object not cathected by instincts loses its dynamogenic value and displacement function. And it is no doubt because the ego is itself cathected by instincts, molding its narcissism from them, that it collaborates so grudgingly in the changes that would be beneficial to it. I have maintained that it is wrong to contrast instincts with the object and that it is through the presence or absence of the object that the instincts come to manifest themselves. *The object is the revealing agent of the instincts.*

Moreover, by giving his final formulations such an extensive character and by opposing the life or love instincts to the destructive instincts, Freud was reducing the instinctual hypothesis to its most general level. It is unnecessary to point out that, in the cultural sphere, it is now more than ever these same factors that are ultimately at work, although admittedly organized differently, behind the complexity of the observable facts as presented to us in individual mental functioning. How are we to account for this correspondence? This would be the subject of another paper.

Freud's concept of instinct, taken as a reference to a psychic life anchored in the body, but in the nature of something already psychic waiting for an object assumed to satisfy it, although unable to avoid disappointing it, demands the development of the representation of that object *and* of the cathexis that includes it in its organization. Its theoretical function is to take account of a paramount link—not only between the body and the object, but also between inside and outside—which would contain the foundations of force and meaning united in a creative matrix. This matrix will give rise, through experience and acknowledgment of the constituents of cultural symbolism, to the subsequent developments, differentiations, and diversifications that will mold the mental life of the individual in the human environment to which he belongs and which he also helps to fashion.

REFERENCES

Brusset, B. 1988. *Psychanalyse du lien: La relation d'objet.* Paris: Le Centurion.
Edelson, M. 1975. *Language and interpretation in psychoanalysis.* New Haven: Yale University Press.

Fairbairn, W. R. D. 1952. *Psychoanalytic studies of the personality.* London: Routledge and Kegan Paul.

Ferenczi, S. 1955. *Final contributions to the problems and methods of psychoanalysis.* London: Hogarth; New York; Basic Books.

Freud, S. 1926. *Inhibitions, symptoms and anxiety, S.E.* 20.

——— 1933. Sándor Ferenczi. *S.E.* 22.

——— 1939. *Moses and monotheism. S.E.* 23.

——— 1940. *An outline of psycho-analysis. S.E.* 23.

Gill, M. 1975. Metapsychology is irrelevant to psychoanalysis. In *The human mind revisited.* Edited by S. Smith. Paris: New International Universities Press.

Green, A. 1988. La pulsion et l'objet, préface à B. Brusset. *Psychanalyse du lien.*

Green, A., et al. 1986. *La pulsion de mort.* Paris: Presses Universitaires de France.

Guntrip, H. 1973. *Personnality structure and human interaction.* London: Hogarth Press.

Hartmann, H. 1964. *Essays on ego psychology.* London: Hogarth Press.

Klein, M. 1949. *The psychoanalysis of children.* London: Hogarth Press.

Kohut, H. 1971. *The analysis of the self.* London: Hogarth Press.

Lacan, J. 1966. *Ecrits.* Paris: Le Seuil; *Ecrits: A Selection.* Translated by A. Sheridan. 1977. London: Tavistock.

Laplanche, J. 1987. *Nouveaux fondements pour la psychanalyse.* Paris: Presses Universitaires de France.

Rank, O. 1929. *The trauma of birth.* London: Kegan Paul, Trench, Trubner.

Schafer, R. 1976. *A new language for psychoanalysis.* New Haven: Yale University Press.

Winnicott, D. W. 1971. *Playing and reality.* London: Tavistock Publications.

Freud:
An Imaginary Dialogue

DAVID ROSENFELD

All the world's a stage,
And all the men and women merely players:
They have their exits and their entrances;
And one man in his time plays many parts . . .
SHAKESPEARE, *As You Like It*

FREUD'S METHOD

D. R.: Let us begin this seminar by trying to express the questions we have about "Analysis Terminable and Interminable."

GERARDO: What was the personal and social background of Freud's treatment of this subject?

ELSA: Freud put it that the main purpose was to think again about what psychoanalysis achieved with patients.

GOYO: It is a taking stock of his life in 1937. With the Nazis already in Germany, perhaps he was thinking that he, as a scientist, was powerless to cure the diseases of cancer, Nazism, and war. So he returned to the destruc-

This paper uses the device of an imaginary dialogue to show that, while there are methods for guiding thought along the route of learning, none of them must ever become a rigid, set schema. Where movement ceases, truth disappears. The emphasis in this approach is less on the conclusions drawn from the discussion than on the interchange stimulated by Freud's ideas—ideas which are so powerful that they challenge one not merely to repeat but to rethink them.

tive instinct, the death drive, and to the possibility of an equilibrium between Eros and Thanatos.

ARTURO: Freud tried to deal with the question in the field of research with which he was familiar—that of psychoanalysis. He was particularly concerned with situations where a complete cure was not achieved. He examined clinical cases familiar to him.

ELSA: He also wondered whether the duration of treatment could be reduced, whether a permanent cure was possible, and whether the patient could be inoculated against falling ill again.

COCO: Although he had so much to say about the possibility of reducing the time, what Freud in fact achieved was to prolong our training analyses from three weeks to six years!·

ELSA: To me it is almost a testament of his life, work, and doubts.

AÍDA: . . . with the aim of locating the obstacles to the cure.

GOYO: Rather than trying to confirm his successes, Freud looked for the obstacles. His work is a model of how a researcher and epistemologist of science should explore an unknown area of which he is still largely ignorant. He demonstrates a specific approach to research in the philosophy of science. Epistemology is concerned with the validation, verification, or refutation of the theories and models we are creating in science. It studies how scientific theories, and scientific knowledge in general, are produced, and investigates the criteria for acceptance or rejection of a theory.

D. R.: It was Karl Popper who introduced and championed the idea that the most important thing in science was not to try to verify but to falsify it. If it was wrong, it could be discarded, but if it was not wrong, it would show its strength by not allowing itself to be refuted. Refuting theories reduces the risk of error. One of the most valuable lessons Freud has taught us is how a scholar ought to confront new problems and difficulties.

GOYO: Another scientist might have called the value of psychoanalytic theory into question in view of the clinical failures. If cure or improvement in the patients is taken as the criterion, it may be felt that the theory is of no use if the patients are not cured . . .

D. R.: Freud believed in his theory and did not abandon it, although, according to orthodox epistemological models, it might seem to have been refuted. Freud's view was that auxiliary or complementary ad hoc hypotheses could be added. These would draw attention to local areas of difficulty without causing the theory to collapse. In this paper one such hypothesis concerns earlier alterations of the ego that he had not taken into account. For Freud, a failure does not mean that a theory is completely wrong. The core of the theory may be correct and may remain intact. Freud would think there were additional factors that had not been sufficiently analyzed or taken into account. Here the epistemologist is Freud would try to find auxiliary hypotheses, either to track down what was at fault or to preserve the core of his theory. Examining what new auxiliary hypotheses could be added was the tactic he adopted in order to find out where previous hypotheses had failed.

GOYO: When we talk about "obstacles," what we mean is that Freud was looking for unknown factors that might be responsible for the peculiarity of the clinical results.

GERARDO: He was more inclined to look for epistemological factors that would enable him to maintain the theory. In seeking auxiliary hypotheses to explain the failures, Freud tried to examine those factors closest to the clinical situation that were responsible for the failures. He had done this long before, in the case of Dora, where, after encountering difficulties, he discovered which factors led to breaking off the analysis or to acting out.

D. R.: Here again, he tried to round off his theory with appropriate additional hypotheses. We could say that Freud was attempting to complement his theory by introducing new models to explain the difficulties. If this tactic were successful, the theory would be enriched. I should like to stress that Freud was not discouraged by the difficulties he met and did not abandon his theory. His attitude was to reexamine the problem, and this led him to important discoveries.

ELSA: I believe that Freud showed partial discouragement when he wrote: " 'Every step forward is only half as big as it looks at first' " (p. 228).

D. R.: As the champion of analytic theory, he did not allow himself to be defeated. He preserved that theory and used it. Thus, in trying to uncover the obstacles responsible for the apparent failures of analysis he rediscovered the existence of primitive and severe alterations of the ego, which he had not previously considered in their full magnitude.

ARTURO: Had he referred to alterations of the ego before?

D. R.: He had spoken of the ego in the 1890s in "The Psychotherapy of Hysteria" (in *Studies on Hysteria*) although he here connected it with an instinctual force. By the time of *The Ego and the Id*, in 1923, it was presented as an organization having specific functions and properties. In 1924, in "Neurosis and Psychosis," he described an ego that restricted, modified, and deformed itself in order to adapt. He had become interested in this question when he considered the structure of the ego in 1914 in "On Narcissism: An Introduction."

ARTURO: I would also mention the book on Leonardo, in which he referred to narcissistic object choice. The ego appeared there as a structure.

BRUNO: We should also not forget Schreber.

ARTURO: We should remember that previously Freud was using a dynamic concept of strength, with repression opposed to the repressed. Now he places more emphasis on defenses altering the actual structure of the ego.

COCO: Another problem Freud discussed was the role of the constitutional versus traumatic aspects. He wrote, "An aetiology of the traumatic sort offers by far the more favourable field for analysis. . . . Only in such cases can one speak of an analysis having been definitively ended" (p.220).

ELSA: In another paragraph, Freud refers to innate modifications of the ego due to defense mechanisms that exacerbate the alterations of the ego.

AÍDA: But here he explains that the ego alterations are of mixed origin. "The aetiology of every neurotic disturbance is, after all, a mixed one. . . . As a rule there is a combination of both factors, the constitutional and the accidental" (p. 220).

TRAUMA

COCO: It seems to me that the word *trauma* as used by Freud here means something external.

ARTURO: Freud's conception of trauma in part V of this paper is not the same as in *Beyond the Pleasure Principle*, where the implication is that the excitation breaks through the stimulus barrier.

BRUNO: I think that here he is talking not about traumatic neurosis in the external sense but about the internal release of a quantity of libido. From this point of view, trauma can be a normal quantity of libido which enters the mental apparatus and surprised the *weak ego*. When he refers here to the *traumatic factor*, he is referring to psychoneurosis.

GOYO: For me, *trauma* means a relation between the entry of a quantity of libido and the defenses. It occurs whenever the sum of excitation overcomes the defensive barriers.

ARTURO: I see it differently. I believe trauma is related here not to internal things but to external ones, as it was in the works on hysteria.

BRUNO: This excitation may come from outside or inside. If it comes from outside, we are dealing with a traumatic neurosis. If it stems from internal sources, we are in the field of the psychoneuroses of traumatic etiology.

ARTURO: I should like to add that the concept of trauma as used in *Beyond the Pleasure Principle* is seen as something that *does* give rise to alterations in the ego. But I would emphasize that in this 1937 paper Freud gave added meaning to his concept of trauma of forty years earlier, when he was talking about hysteria.

COCO: You say that this sum of excitation comes from outside only . . .

ARTURO: But I wonder if the developments that took place in experience were paralleled in theory. In this seminar I stand for the person who doubts that theories evolve with the passage of time. Might it not be that a theory regresses instead of advancing in a straight line?

GERARDO: I, on the other hand, am the one in this group who thinks that the theories evolve and grow along a straight line of development.

D. R.: I think that there are some arguments about Freud in which people forget that they are talking about different thoughts, periods, and times.

JEAN PAUL: All thought goes through different periods of growth and retreat—the process is dialectical.

GOYO: What an interesting methodological problem! I believe that this discussion concretely illustrates the ebb and flow in the history of a theory, and in general the methodology of the sciences . . .

D. R.: The relation between the strengths of the trauma and of the ego is a dialectical one. The concept of interrelated structures and substructures and the dualistic dialectic of conflicts in Freud's work are fundamental.

FOOD FOR THOUGHT

ARTURO: In "The Psychotherapy of Hysteria," Freud took another look at his method of treatment and catharsis, and it was only forty years later that he discovered that a change in the technical approach to interpretation was necessary. If only the id (and not the ego) is interpreted, "we have interpreted only for ourselves not for the patient" (p. 238).

D. R.: As regards technique and the formulation of interpretations, what you say suggests to me that sometimes the fact a message is given does not mean that it is received, listened to, classified, understood, or decoded by the recipient. Present-day communications theory has thrown a great deal of light on the specific problems involved.

AÍDA: What you are saying is there in Freud's text: "We have increased his knowledge, but altered nothing else in him" (p. 233).

JEAN PAUL: He already had something to say about this in the papers on technique. He was now adding a new structural understanding to it.

GOYO: This point is one of the "obstacles" to the cure, which we may identify as one of the themes of communication theory. To return to what you were saying, Freud's point is that the theories and techniques were not bad, but they were insufficiently complete for the patient to acquire knowledge. As the analyst's theoretical knowledge increases, so he is able to modify his technique and capability.

D. R: Yes, but consider what a difficult job we have. After all, we not only have to ensure that the patient acquires a certain knowledge but we must also judge the patient's own theories about himself. The epistemology of the psychoanalyst is much more active than that of the physicist, who does not have this problem. Psychoanalysis raises a fascinating epistemological problem because, in addition to what happens in other sciences, where the scientist acts on the material and observes how it responds, the psychoanalyst performs a specific epistemological function. He causes the patient to know something and to evaluate the knowledge he has acquired.

COCO: This is complicated, because he is also involved as a person in this function.

GERARDO: This is one of the obstacles that Freud includes under the wider heading of "obstacles to the treatment."

AÍDA: In other words, it again becomes clear that obstacles are not a result of mistakes in psychoanalytic theory, but an indication of areas of research still to be carried out. These include the limitations of the therapist as a person.

GOYO: Freud was an epistemologist who modified the auxiliary hypotheses of psychoanalysis in order to preserve a theory. It was these auxiliary hypotheses which were not complete—for instance, once the childhood of the Wolf Man, his archaic narcissism, his paranoid regressions, and his aggression were reviewed and reconceptualized, a much wider and more severe psychopathology was uncovered.

D. R.: It was the same with Newton. There is no need to change Newton's theory because someone suddenly discovers a part of the sky that he did not investigate sufficiently, and in which there is a disturbing mass. This is not a flaw in the theory but a new piece of information to be included, one which will be taken into account in future calculations. If we relate this to clinical practice, the issues relate to prior alterations of the ego which had not yet been discovered and had as a consequence not been studied. To characterize this unknown factor, it is necessary to make new hypotheses. The appropriate epistemological tactic is one that will enable us to penetrate further into this unknown factor. One obstacle to this is the name we give to what is not yet known and has not yet been studied, and which changes the outcome of our predictions.

COCO: How many psychoanalysts and scientists have believed they already knew everything!

ELSA: Again and again there is the discovery of something new that can be appropriately incorporated into one's own theory.

GERARDO: We may even believe Freud's metapsychology may have been an enterprise of theoretical creation—that he created a metapsychology for each individual or particular type of patient. So we would have the conscious–unconscious dichotomy for hysterics; ego, superego, and id for melancholics, depressives, schizoid patients, and so forth.

ELSA: Sometimes not even the creators themselves can appreciate the full theoretical implications of their own discoveries.

D. R.: Something like that happened to Einstein. Revolutionary as he was, when other Heisenberg and followers argued, on the basis of the master's ideas, that the ultimate laws of the universe might be probabilistic and not deterministic, Einstein turned aside and pronounced the famous sentence "God does not play dice."

COCO: There is much that we still do not know.

WILLIAM: "There are more things in heaven and earth . . . ."

AÍDA: When Freud describes resistances to the uncovering of resistances, he is theorizing about something that was hitherto unknown.

ARTURO: Not entirely. In *Inhibitions, Symptoms and Anxiety* he describes one of the ego resistances.

AÍDA: The relevant quotation from "Analysis Terminable and Interminable" is, "we should not reckon on meeting with a resistance against the uncovering of resistances. But what happens is this. . . . The ego ceases to support our efforts at uncovering the id" (p. 239).

BRUNO: This paper was used as a foundation for subsequent theories, such as Hartmann's idea of ego development, and the concepts of autonomy, changing states of ego organization, adaptation, perception and so on discussed by Hartmann and by Anna Freud in her book *The Ego and Mechanisms of Defence*, quoted in Freud's paper.

D. R.: According to Blum (1987), other authors in the United States stress the importance of this work in stimulating their ideas on and interest in pathogenesis and theories of evolutionary development.

AÍDA: While others—for instance, Melanie Klein—emphasize earlier aspects of childhood object relations.

ANALYZABILITY

D. R.: What sort of patients was Freud referring to, and what sort of analysts was he thinking of?

GERARDO: The patients I see in my hospital practice—borderline, psychotics, and drug addicts—are, I believe, different from the ones Freud is referring to here.

ARTURO: But let us remember that Freud taught us about serious pathologies in regard to such cases as those of Schreber, the Rat Man, and the Wolf Man.

D. R.: What concept of analyzability does each of you have in mind?

AÍDA: What Freud says is that a patient might not be amenable to analysis owing to a structural alteration of the ego.

GOYO: In addition to the criteria of analyzability given by Freud, we now have the ability, fifty years later, to make new and better diagnoses with the new theoretical knowledge we have. A psychosomatic clinical picture, a neurosis, a borderline case, and a temporary psychosis are not the same thing.

AÍDA: I am surprised Freud did not include here theoretical concepts such as psychosomatic illnesses and nonverbal languages.

ARTURO: It seems to me that he did discuss psychosomatic illness to some extent in the work on President Wilson.

D. R.: Returning to the subject of the analyzability (or otherwise) of a patient, I believe that today we know more about the concepts of intersystemic and intrasystemic conflict, weakness of the ego, negative therapeutic reactions (whether true or false), and primitive forms of transference, sometimes called delusional, psychotic, or highly regressive transferences.

AÍDA: As someone interested in child analysis, I should like to add that, by helping us to locate or to date conflicts within the ego in the patient's development, this paper was partly responsible for allowing child analyses to begin at an earlier age. This changed our ideas about analyzability and prognosis.

GERARDO: It had the same effect on the psychoses.

AÍDA: I should like to ask a question about the part of the paper where Freud says, "In states of acute crisis analysis is to all intents and purposes unusable" (p. 232).

COCO: Is he referring to acute internal states (for example, an ego absorbed in mourning), or to acute external situations, or to acute psychotic crises?

ARTURO: There is a reference in "The Psychotherapy of Hysteria" to the clinical pictures of acute hysteria. Freud had the feeling that everything he said was diluted for patients in the midst of these acute symptoms. However, he seems to wonder whether treatment in acute states prevents the appearance of subsequent symptoms.

GERARDO: On the subject of acute psychosis, if I may answer you, I would say that we are now able to confront and investigate episodes of acute psychosis with more theoretical and technical knowledge than we had fifty years ago. The work of Herbert Rosenfeld and Harold Searles clearly illustrates the usefulness of strictly psychoanalytic interpretations in dealing with psychotic patients. Might this not indicate a change in the concept of analyzability since 1937?

D. R.: Since this paper makes us think about the concept of analyzability, I should like to refer to the developments of communications theory by Bateson, Watzlawick, and Liberman. It was Liberman who applied this to psychoanalysis, maintaining that the concept of analyzability should not be considered from the point of view of the diagnosis of a single person but depended on the possibility of establishing good communication between the members of the analytical couple. Some analysts, owing to their personal characteristics and theoretical knowledge, may not perform well with some patients.

AÍDA: Do you think this paper encouraged the analysis of psychotic or very disturbed children?

D. R.: I would say yes, that it did so by encouraging the analysis of earlier disturbances and of alterations of the ego. My interest is aroused by Freud's statement that these resistances are "*separated off* [italics added] within the ego" (p.239). In the German edition the word here translated as "separated off" is *gesondert*. Freud does not use instead the word *Spaltung*, which is closer to dissociation or splitting. I want to stress this point because it touches on a field of research that particularly fascinates me — that of parts which remain *encapsulated but separated off within the ego*. This relates to the area of autism and infantile psychosis and especially to encapsulated autistic nuclei which, according to some recent conceptions, survive in adult patients. These separated nuclei may reappear in a different way from aspects that have been dissociated or split off. This is a mechanism that may define new forms of diagnosis in clinical practice.

FEELINGS, AFFECTS, PASSIONS, AND ILLNESSES

AÍDA: The negative therapeutic reaction as an *obstacle* which appears before any progress in the treatment is a clear phenomenon about which there can be no argument.

D. R.: Provided that you can detect *when* there is progress — that, at any rate, you have your own personal definition. The analyst does not always notice negative therapeutic reactions, because very often they take silent, hidden forms. We are not dealing with concrete, static facts like those of physics. In other words, any concept is relative and depends on the definition given to it by the analyst in the clinical field. The same thing happens with the concept of acting out. This is not a concrete fact, a "thing-in-itself." It is only a definition which I give in the psychoanalytical field to an *action* performed by the patient. If I then define it, I add it to the theoretical baggage I carry with me. Learn to think that everything is relative . . .

AÍDA: But the negative therapeutic reaction is an obstacle . . .

D. R.: No, *I insist on the relativity of the concept.* For example, the negative therapeutic reaction may be a step forward in cases of obsessional character pathology, in silent schizoid states, and in patients who discover arguing is not the same thing as killing. In the psychoses, apparent negative therapeutic reactions may be attempts to preserve a little piece of the self reconstructed in the treatment. The patient is afraid he may be robbed of this. In a reanalysis, it may be a violent reaction against the previous therapist. This last type of negative therapeutic reaction can, if diagnosed early, be overcome.

AÍDA: We can expand from the problems of Ferenczi with his ex-analyst Freud to the problems of *termination of analyses* and *training analyses*.

BRUNO: Yes. A key point is that what the analyst received in his own analysis must continue to operate within him. Freud says, "But we reckon on the stimuli that he has received in his own analysis not ceasing when it ends and on the processes of remodelling the ego continuing spontaneously" (p. 249).

D. R.: An analysis may be *terminable* for the therapist but *interminable* in the mind of the patient.

GERARDO: Changes in the personal or scientific life of a psychoanalyst usually cause him to think again about the values he received from his own past analysis. Even the good aspects of this treatment may be called into question.

COCO: During the Argentinian military dictatorship around 1977, patients and therapists sometimes had opposing, dissimilar, or contrary political opinions.

ELSA: Something like that happened to psychoanalysts in 1937 in the Berlin Society, with the Nazis in power.

GOYO: I find this beautiful sentence remarkable, "And finally we must not forget that the analytic relationship is based on a love of truth—that is, on a recognition of reality—and that it precludes any kind of sham or deceit (p. 248).

D. R.: Being honest as a therapist means teaching people not to falsify reality.

WILLIAM: "This above all: to thine own self be true and it must follow, as the night the day, thou canst not then be false to any man . . ."

COCO: On behalf of the neurotics—sorry, of the psychoanalysts, as we are all a bit neurotic—I should like to draw attention to this sentence: "Our aim will not be to rub off every peculiarity of human character for the sake of a schematic 'normality,' nor yet to demand that the person who has been 'thoroughly analysed' shall feel no passions and develop no internal conflicts" (p. 250).

WILLIAM: "Have we not eyes? Have we not hands, organs, dimensions, senses, affections, passions? Fed with the same food, subject to the same diseases, healed by the same means, warmed and cooled by the same winter and summer? If you prick us, do we not bleed? If you tickle us, do we not laugh?"

D. R.: As Lagache wrote, the notion of conflict is inherent in psychic structure. We need to know simply that we are human beings but with a very special quality. When Freud speaks of the capacity for introspection and self-observation, I think this is one of the most important things for us, as well as having the capacity to learn to learn.

GOYO: After all, if the analyst does not have an epistemophilic function, if he has no curiosity and imagination and is incapable of learning to learn, his capacity for psychoanalytic research will be greatly reduced.

ELSA: What will be the future of research?

D. R.: We are talking about the therapist. I believe that psychoanalysts must be prepared to acquire new knowledge and *greater tolerance of the impact* of severely disturbed patients in long treatments. The future of analysis at the clinical level calls for a greater capacity to study the very primitive types of transferences called psychotic, delusional, or highly regressed, which give rise to very strange and intense *countertransference* effects in therapists. These are seen particularly with regressed, borderline, highly disturbed, psychotic, and drug-addicted patients.

BRUNO: How does this differ from the neurotic transference?

D. R.: The psychotic transference is quantitatively much more intense than other types of transference. Qualitatively it has more delusional characteristics than in the neuroses. *Psychotic transference* is the patient's total and absolute conviction about a delusional belief which he has concerning his therapist and—more important—acts out in consequence. "Acting out in consequence" is important in cases where this psychotic transference is not manifested openly but is hidden or silent and detectable only from its effects.

COCO: How many things we have to learn . . .

D. R.: The most important thing is human sensitivity and common sense. Unfortunately, it seems to me that these cannot be learned in psychoanalytic seminars.

BRUNO: Freud makes us think of the *countertransference.*

D. R.: Because *empathy*—being able to feel with the patient—is one thing, while analytic technique, in which it is important *not* to make confessions, is another. We have to use our feelings simply as a signal for understanding, followed by decoding them and putting them into words with the appropriate timing. That is how we explain some aspects of the term *countertransference*.

GERARDO: The analyst also must have undergone technical training and must not use patients for the projection of his own problems, as Freud clearly states in his paper. He says, "It seems that a number of analysts learn to make use of defensive mechanisms which allow them to divert the implications and demands of analysis from themselves (probably by directing them on to other people) . . ." (p. 249).

WILLIAM: "By the fool multitude, that choose by show, not learning more than the fond eye doth teach, which pries not the interior, but, like the martlet, builds in the weather on the outward wall . . ."

BEFORE AND AFTER

COCO: At the time Freud was working on the case of the Wolf Man, was he looking for a traumatic origin for the disturbance?

D. R.: Yes, but something else as well. He was also looking for the symptom as a transaction that he could go on investigating, step by step, in the patient's childhood. He described the Wolf Man's infantile sexual wishes, primal scene and castration fantasies. "Instincts and their Vicissitudes" was based partly on what Freud learned from the Wolf Man.

GOYO: Here again we see how a theory of high general level is the result of observations with a specific patient or group of patients.

COCO: How was Freud to conceptualize this in 1937?

ARTURO: In *Inhibitions, Symptoms and Anxiety* he took another look at the neurosis of the Wolf Man from the point of his theory of anxiety, his new theory of conflict, and a new theory of defense. He shifted to a new psychopathological conception in 1937.

BRUNO: So in 1937 Freud had more to say about the ego in the case of the Wolf Man. The attempt to coordinate the demands of id, superego, and external world, and the failure of the ego to accomplish this coordination, caused him to locate this failure at an earlier developmental stage. He shifted from symptom analysis to the study of pathology more connected with the ego.

AÍDA: He was now thinking in terms of the life and death instincts. This interplay between Eros and Thanatos is one of the factors determining prognosis.

D. R.: We have just seen how Freud modified the description of the conflict from the structural point of view and from that of instinctual conflict. He did not speak of a conflict between narcissistic libido and object libido, but of a conflict between Eros and Thanatos. He did not say that the passivity of the Wolf Man gave rise to his masochistic attitudes, but spoke of primary masochism.

ARTURO: The masochism of the Wolf Man seems in 1937 to be within the bedrock, that is, connected with the intensity of the drives and the innate structure of the ego. It is an apparent "obstacle" to cure.

GOYO: In this way he explains how the idea one has of a patient and his prognosis may change as the frame of reference and the theories gradually change and as new knowledge is acquired.

JEAN PAUL: How would you now study the Wolf Man, Dr. R.?

D. R.: I would prefer to look at the transference relationship between the patient and the therapist and to study Freud's countertransference reactions (if I could find them) in his notes. I have already done this with the material of the Rat Man in a paper on the handling of resistances. An example of my approach might be the speculation that the Wolf Man's fantasy of having an operation on his nose was due to his confusing himself with Freud and wanting to have an operation on his face just as at the time surgery was being performed on Freud's mouth tumor.

WILLIAM: "Reality could be worse than any dream."

TERMINATION

ELSA: Freud's concept of a natural end to an analysis makes one think. Did it have just one meaning, or a large number of different ones?

JEAN PAUL: Each school or geographical area may have a different way of conceiving of it and theorizing about it, or may adopt different criteria relating to the development of an analysis. It is rather difficult to distinguish clearly between the idea of a phase of termination or concepts about it, and the notion of a natural end. I think they are two aspects of one and the same problem.

D. R.: Yes, for some schools, the aim may be to attain genitality. For others, it is to work through what the Kleinians call the depressive position. Others take it to be the resolution of symbiosis and nondifferentiation. Some have the criterion of a self-sufficient ego structure with appropriate defenses, while others refer to the possibility of expression in words. Then there are those for whom the termination will be detectable in the analytical transference, with the linguistic possibility of measuring the greater flow of information and the increased linguistic transmission of affects in human communication. Others look for indications of changes in phonology and the music of the voice in analytic terminations. All this is extremely interesting. And we all know about working through, dreaming, insight, and so on.

GERARDO: Some of us have severely disturbed patients in psychoanalytic treatment. We have learned *to treat patients for a much longer time*. So the criteria for *termination* are also connected with the severity of the psychopathology.

D. R.: Not all patients can separate and introject. For some separation may be equated with a catastrophe, with the end of the world, with being flogged, with no longer having a skin and being exposed in their rawness. But this is discovered after many years, with subtle linguistic clues which may in analysis appear once or twice a year, or in psychosomatic language. We can theorize about it in many ways. But treatments extending over many years are necessary. There is much that we still do not know.

THE PENDULUM

ARTURO: It seems to me that when Freud speaks of alterations of the ego he includes technical points he has suggested before: "It sometimes turns out that the ego has paid too high a price for the services they render it" (p. 237).

ELSA: In the Dora analysis Freud says that we concern ourselves first with the unconscious and then with the ego, while on other occasions we deal with resistance. He gradually reconceptualizes the entire model, which is nothing more nor less than the psychoanalysis he is creating, developing dialectically.

BRUNO: It is clear that defenses appear that do not oppose the ego or the repressed but rather alter the structure of the ego itself. This point seems fundamental to me.

COCO: I do not understand this business of the pendulum (p. 238) . . .

AÍDA: I believe he is saying that, in one and the same treatment, and with one and the same patient, you proceed from resistance to the repressed, from the repressed to resistance, or, if you like, to the defense mechanisms, which appear on the surface. There is an ebb and flow.

GOYO: Originally the protagonists were the id and infantile sexuality. However, in 1937 we have an interplay between the ego and the id. Hence the pendulum. And what about the superego?

ARTURO: It seems to me that it is the same as Freud described in *The Ego and the Id*. I do not think it has been greatly changed. The superego sinks more into the id.

BRUNO: May I say that "impoverished" does not mean "altered." In 1937, Freud speaks of *alterations*. I think he is indicating something else, namely the type of alterations he described in "Neurosis and Psychosis" and in "Splitting of the Ego in the Process of Defence." I am quite certain that by 1937 he was thinking more about the actual structure of the ego.

ARTURO: I still think that this is explained—indeed, explained better—in "The Psychotherapy of Hysteria."

D. R.: We are not dealing with rigid models. I believe the fact that he sometimes uses the same words does not imply that they mean the same thing. After all, in the context of models at different levels the same word comes to form part of the structure of a more complex and more dynamic model and acquires a different meaning.

GOYO: I thought that previously it was a matter of making the unconscious conscious. Not now. Now Freud says that making a conflict conscious is not enough to resolve it, and that something new arises, "new resistances in the ego"—resistances to the uncovering of resistances.

ARTURO: This is also connected with *Inhibitions, Symptoms and Anxiety*, where he speaks of the five types of resistance. One of these, the *superego resistance*, is connected with the unconscious sense of guilt and related to the negative therapeutic reaction, which is mentioned in this paper as one of the obstacles to cure.

D. R.: The fifth type of resistance, the *id resistance*, is a theoretical abstraction, but it may be observed in clinical practice in, for example, a closed circuit of communication (called *entropy* by some authors), which is repeated between the patient and the therapist.

TERMINATION, DISTORTIONS, RELATIVITY

JEAN PAUL: Do the effects observed in the termination of therapeutic analysis differ from those in training analyses?

AÍDA: What happened with Ferenczi and his reproaches to Freud? What were they about? A failure to diagnose? A premature termination, as the analysis lasted only a short time? Was it a typical problem of an unresolved termination, or a negative therapeutic reaction? Ferenczi seems to have been very confused when he looked after, caressed, and kissed his patients.

D. R.: Ferenczi was then seriously confusing himself with Freud, himself with patients, and his own adult needs with his infantile needs. He was confusing love and hate, who he was and who the other was. It is rather like the fusion of a baby with its mother, or like being in love. A poet put it much better: "One half of me is yours, the other half mine own." I would say, "but if mine, then yours, and so all yours."

Ferenczi's analysis with Freud may be an example of semantic distortion in which the decision to dismiss a patient is something that the analyst regards as a reasonable decision. However, the patient may distort it and experience it as if his therapist is rejecting him or no longer loves him.

GERARDO: Semantic distortion is the distortion that takes place in the meaning of the treatment.

AÍDA: In other words, what is *terminable* for the therapist may be recoded by the patient (although at more infantile, primitive, and hidden levels) into a totally different meaning.

D. R.: We may think this when we come to the vague and ambiguous term *natural end* used by Freud. "Natural" for what part of the patient, we wonder? For an adult part, it may represent something quite different from its meaning for an infantile or undifferentiated and symbiotic part. The parts of the mind that live at primitive levels of nondifferentiation, at levels of confusion and symbiosis, cannot understand the concept of the *natural end*. They find it incomprehensible and in some cases even transform it delusionally into an attack on their infantile needs.

COCO: That is what happened to Ferenczi with Freud at the end of his treatment.

D. R.: What is terminable for the therapist may not be so for the patient who, in some parts of his mind, wishes to fulfill or to act out infantile needs which have never been resolved.

ELSA: Didn't the same thing happen with the Wolf Man's termination?

GERARDO: He may have felt well looked after by Freud, thanks to the collections of money organized to help him, and we may look from this new point of view at the fact that he concealed his recovery of his inheritance and the family jewels. It is not that he was dishonest or lying or concealing. These are *ethical* and not psychoanalytic ideas. In psychoanalytic terms, his action expresses his wish to continue being looked after in a symbiotic relationship, or one in which the infant is supported by the mother for a longer period than normal.

D. R.: What you say may be right. Another clinical diagnosis may even be possible in regard to the Wolf Man. But what interests me above all is *to hold on to doubts, and not to things that are cut and dried.* We should realize that in very disturbed patients there are areas involving object relations that are highly regressive, obscure, and encapsulated. These are areas that are still largely unknown to us. The best form of learning is to begin to recognize what we do not yet know.

JEAN PAUL: We can create a model to represent what we do not yet know. We can imagine that the unknown is behind a wall and is not visible. Then we can explain the obstacles by additional hypotheses.

GOYO: Each model is a personal creation, but many people confuse the model with absolute, total, and unchangeable truth. The model, included in a context of higher-level hypotheses, serves for theory formation.

ARTURO: So when Freud talks about the unmodifiable bedrock of biology, is that a model?

D. R.: Strictly speaking, it is a metaphor. But if we interpret it as a psychological model and use it as Freud does, in a psychological sense, whether as penis envy or masculine protest, it is useful to me, because it puts the question on the psychological level, and this is my limited area of psychoanalytic work.

LEARNING

AÍDA: I feel more comfortable if I have a firm theory with a solid structure that tells me what I should do.

GERARDO: If I can tolerate the idea that there are things I do not know, I feel more humble toward the patient and have a greater desire to learn.

GOYO: A third solution may be to modify one's theories, but the point is to be able to tolerate change; otherwise one is in the position the opponents of Galileo were in when he wanted to change a theory. Their reply to him was that they could see no need to look through the telescope because the structure of the universe and the celestial spheres had already been completely explained by the master, Aristotle.

D. R.: Each of you three represents a model of the dialectical movement of learning: a person striving and wishing for an orderly, more stable and rigid theory; a person able to doubt or to have humility in the face of not knowing; and a person capable of seeking a new approach, a new theory. Each of you is expressing *different phases* of learning, through which we all pass.

It is as Sartre put it about freedom: Freedom is a process, a constant struggle, a goal which one tries to achieve. To say that one is already free, that one has total liberty, is just as rash as to say, in the practice of psychoanalysis, that one already knows everything and that there is nothing more to be learned.

JEAN PAUL: To return to the matter of theory, I think that theory is one thing, whereas the clinical use that may be made of it in psychoanalysis is another.

ELSA: The explanations supplied by a theory may be very wide-ranging and useful, but a theory may be unable to explain all the patients to whom it is applied.

D. R: It is impossible to explain all patients by a single theory. But some particular theory may be more applicable to the understanding of a larger number of patients.

COCO: So in practice it is not so easy to apply a single theory equally to all patients.

D. R.: I should say that there is a general psychoanalytic theory which serves as a foundation for the advancing of new, additional hypotheses. But the additional hypotheses to be formed for particular clinical cases must not be general ones applicable to all clinical cases.

COCO: It is not so easy . . .

WILLIAM : "If to do were as easy as to know what were good to do, chapels had been churches, and poor men's cottages princes' palaces. . . ."

REFERENCES

Bateson, G., and Jackson, D. 1964. In *Disorders of communication*, 270–83. Research Publications. Association for Research in Nervous and Mental Disease.

Blum, H. 1987. Analysis terminable and interminable: A half-century retrospective. *Int. J. Psycho-Anal.*, vol. 78, no. 1.

Freud, A. 1936. *The ego and the mechanisms of defence*. New York: International Universities Press.

Freud, S. 1895. The psychotherapy of hysteria. In *Studies on hysteria. S.E.* 2.

———. 1895. *Studies on hysteria. S.E.* 2

———. 1905. Fragment of an analysis of a case of hysteria. *S.E.* 7.

———. 1909. Notes upon a case of obsessional neurosis. *S.E.* 10.

———. 1911. Psycho-analytic notes on an autobiographical account of a case of paranoia. *S.E.* 12.

———. 1914. On narcissism. *S.E.* 14.

———. 1915. Instincts and their vicissitudes. *S.E.* 14.

———. 1918. From the history of an infantile neurosis. *S.E.* 17.

———. 1920. *Beyond the pleasure principle. S.E.* 18.

———. 1923. *The ego and the id. S.E.* 19.

———. 1924. Neurosis and psychosis. *S.E.* 19.

———. 1926. *Inhibition, symptoms and anxiety. S.E.* 20.

———. 1937. Analysis terminable and interminable. *S.E.* 23.

———. 1940. Splitting of the ego in the process of defence. *S.E.* 23.

Freud, S., and Bullitt, W. C. 1967. *Thomas Woodrow Wilson: A psychological study*. London: Weidenfeld and Nicolson.

Hartmann, H. 1964. *Essays on ego psychology*. London: Hogarth Press.

Jones, E. 1962. *Sigmund Freud: Life and work*. London: Hogarth Press.

Klein, M. 1975. *Envy and gratitude, and other works*. London: Hogarth Press.

Lagache, D. 1961. La psychanalyse et la structure de la personalité. In *La psychanalyse* 6.

Liberman, D. 1983. *Lingüistica, interacción comunicativa y proceso psicoanalytico*. Buenos Aires: Galerna–Nueva Visión.

Popper, K. 1965. *Conjectures and refutations: The growth of scientific knowledge*. New York: Basic Books.

Rosenfeld, D. (1986). Identification and its vicissitudes in relation to the Nazi phenomenon. *Int. J. Psycho-Anal.* 67:53–64.

———. (1988). *Psychoanalysis and groups: History and dialectic.* London: Karnac Books.

———. 1989. Handling of resistances in adult patients. *Int. J. Psycho-Anal.* 61:71–83.

———. (1990). *Master clinicians on treating the regressed patient: Psychotic body image.* Edited by L. Bryce Boyer and Peter Giovacchini. Northvale, N.J.: Jason Aronson.

Rosenfeld, H. 1987. *Impasse and interpretation.* London: Tavistock.

Sartre, Jean-Paul. 1960. *Critique de la raison dialectique.* Paris: Gallimard.

Searles, H. 1979. *Countertransference and related subjects.* New York: International Universities Press.

Shakespeare, William. *The complete works.* Annotated. The Globe Illustrated Shakespeare Greenwich House. New York: Crown, 1979.

Watzlawick, P.; Veavin, J.; and Jackson. 1967. *Pragmatics of human communication.* New York: W. W. Norton.

List of
Contributors

JACOB A. ARLOW is clinical professor of psychiatry at New York University College of Medicine. He is a member of the New York Psychoanalytic Society, the Psychoanalytic Association of New York, and the the Association for Psychoanalytic Medicine (honorary). He is a past president of the American Psychoanalytic Association and was formerly editor-in-chief of the *Psychoanalytic Quarterly*.

ARNOLD M. COOPER is professor of psychiatry at New York Hospital-Cornell Medical Center and supervising and training psychoanalyst at Columbia University Center for Psychoanalytic Training and Research. He is past president of the American Psychoanalytic Association, past vice-president of the IPA, and is currently an associate secretary of the IPA. He is a co-editor of *Psychoanalysis: Toward the Second Century*.

TERTTU ESKELINEN DE FOLCH is training analyst at the Spanish Psychoanalytical Society. She is vice-president of the European Psychoanalytic Federation and a former director of the Psychoanalytic Institute of Barcelona. She was also formerly editor of the *Bulletin* of the European Psychoanalytic Federation.

PETER FONAGY is senior lecturer in psychology, University of London; coordinator of research at the Anna Freud Centre, Hampstead; the Freud Memorial Professor Designate, University College London; a member of the British Psychoanalytical Society; and associate secretary, IPA. He is the author of two monographs with A. C. Higgitt, *Personality and Clinical Practice* and *Benzediazepene Dependence*.

ANDRÉ GREEN is a former director of the Paris Psychoanalytic Institute and past president of the Paris Psychoanalytic Society. He also held the Freud Memorial Chair, University College London, and has served as vice president of the IPA. His books include *On Private Madness* and *Le Discours Vivant*.

HARALD LEUPOLD-LÖWENTHAL is university docent in the University of Vienna, president of the Sigmund Freud Society, Vienna, and a training and supervising analyst in the Viennese Psychoanalytical Society.

A. L. BENTO MOSTARDEIRO is president of the Mário Martins Institute, where he is also professor and supervisor of the Psychiatric Specialization Program and the Psychotherapy Training Program. He is an associate member of the Porto Alegre Psychoanalytic Society. Formerly, he was professor of psychiatry at the Federal University of Rio Grande do Sul, Brazil.

ETHEL S. PERSON is director and training and supervising analyst at Columbia University Center for Psychoanalytic Training and Research and professor of clinical psychiatry at College of Physicians & Surgeons of Columbia University. She is chairman of the Publications Committee of the IPA and author of *Dreams of Love and Fateful Encounters: The Power of Romantic Passion*.

DAVID ROSENFELD is training analyst and professor of psychopathology of psychosis at Buenos Aires Psychoanalytic Society. He is former professor of psychoanalysis and semiotics at the University (Buenos Aires). He has authored a recent book *Psychoanalysis and Groups. History and Dialectis.*

JOSEPH SANDLER is the Freud Memorial Professor of Psychoanalysis and director of the Psychoanalysis Unit, the University of London. He is training and supervising analyst at the British Psychoanalytical Society and president of the IPA.

DAVID ZIMMERMANN is director and professor of the Psychotherapy Training Program, as well as director and professor of Psychiatric Specialization Program, Mário Martins Institute. He is a past president of the Brazilian Psychiatric Association and has served as vice-president and associate secretary of IPA. His most recent book is *Relações da Psicanalise com Analistas Didatas Intituiçoes e Pacientes*.

Index